Other Books by Patrick Shaub
Flying the Lifeline:
Volume 1, Marine Helicopter Pilot
Volume 2, Scene Call
Volume 3, Don't Spare the Horses

MAKE MONEY
WITH DRONES

MAKE MONEY WITH DRONES

Learn the steps to starting your own drone based business?

PATRICK R. SHAUB

Printed in the United States of America

ISBN 10: 1533153728
ISBN 13: 9781533153722
Library of Congress Control Number: 2016907943
CreateSpace Independent Publishing Platform
North Charleston, South Carolina

DON'T MISS THIS OPPORTUNITY!

D rones are as important a change in technology as laptops and cell phones were in the past. Drones _will_ change the way we live our lives. If you've picked up this book, chances are you already know that. If not, I encourage you to join the leading edge of the tsunami of opportunity working with drones represents. Find out how to start a drone-based business. This book provides you with the steps to lead the pack and **Make Money With Drones.** Inside this book you'll find exciting opportunity you can seize, and directions for taking the steps to start a safe, legal and successful drone-based business of your own. You'll find questions you should ask before starting your journey, and answers to those questions that will make the path to success in this brand new business easier to follow.

If you're already in some aspect of the drone business, this book will point out opportunities to expand that business into places you've never thought of before. If this book is not for you, chances are that you know someone who will appreciate a copy. If you know someone who is imaginative and innovative and just looking for an opportunity to engage in something where their enthusiasm can be thoroughly spent, **Make**

Money with Drones is for them. This book is a guide that every pioneer stepping into the drone industry will appreciate.

Fair Winds!

Patrick Shaub
President, "Beeline Drones"
1111 Highland Hills Drive
Marble Falls, Texas 786545
512-755-0615
http://beelinedrones.com

FOREWORD

After a lifetime of piloting both rotor wing and fixed wing aircraft, Patrick Shaub has morphed into the sUAS drone business world. He has done his homework and received an A+ grade. If you have a mere suspicion of interest in the drone business world, read this book and you will be hooked. Shaub has put a lot of research and forethought into his "Make Money with Drones" book. He understands the multitude of industry service/sales channels out there today. Being able to offer multiple drone services is critical to creating multiple revenue streams. Having been in this business for over 13 years I understand how networking and social media becomes the start-up drone businesses gorilla marketing arm. Pat agrees. Start out with just one application and grow as you go. The drone *service* market is wide open globally & nationwide! Patrick rolls up his sleeves and digs into the nuts & bolts of this game changing industry. You should too!

Hoot Gibson
Airborne Geospatial Services & Solutions

AROW

"MAKE MONEY WITH DRONES!"

WHY WOULD I WANT TO START A BUSINESS WITH DRONES?

...THEY CHANGED THE WAY WE LIVE.

Imagine its 1980 and you're asking yourself, "Why would I want to start a business with cellular phones?" Or it's the 1990s and you ask, "Why would I want to get involved in a business with laptop computers?" Or it's 2001 and you ask, "Why would I want to get involved in business on the Internet?" Today everybody owns a cell phone, *and* some form of portable computer and they are all connected to the Internet. But back when they were where drones are today, few could have imagined the incredible capabilities and opportunities that lay ahead in the introduction of those advances in technology.

Fortunate for the people back then who had a little imagination, savvy and the will to work people became rich starting cell phone companies, and miniature computer businesses. The same kind of people got involved at the outset with the Internet. We know the names of some of these people today because they changed the way we live and because they are now among the über-wealthy. Many of those same smart people today are getting *heavily* involved in drones.

Now here *you* are, standing on the cusp of the next world-changing technology revolution asking yourself if you should reach out and grab an opportunity of a lifetime. Drones are already changing the world. You should be one of the people to seize the opportunities wide open at the moment, to get involved with drones. And *that* is why you should want to start a drone-based business.

WHAT IS A DRONE?

Simply: a "drone" is a remote controlled, pilotless aircraft. A drone can be either fixed-wing (like an airplane) or rotary wing (like a helicopter). Because they fly like airplanes and helicopters, a drone can do many of the same things airplanes and helicopters can do. Because they're unmanned they can do many things manned aircraft can't do, or no one would want to do with a manned aircraft. Like get shot down, for example.

Early drones were used by the military as aerial targets. Sometimes they were expressly built for that use. Often though, drones were outdated military aircraft rigged with remote controls. Early drones trained gunners or got shot down by various guns and missiles under development. That kind of military drone is still being flown today. So too are military 'killer drones' we're all reading about in the news. When a carload of terrorists on a remote desert road suddenly gets struck out of nowhere by a missile or bomb, military 'killer drones' are often the culprit. They have appropriate names like "Reaper" or "Predator." But military drones are not what this book is about.

...THESE ADVANCES BEGINS THE AGE OF WHAT IS BECOMING KNOWN AS, "ELECTRIC AVIATION."

This book is about starting businesses with "Unmanned Aerial Systems" (UAS)." That's what the US Federal Aviation Administration (FAA) calls them. UAS aircraft are categorized by the FAA according to weight. Small drones or (sUAS) weigh less than 55 pounds. Starting a business with these small drones is the primary focus of this book. The principles apply to businesses with larger drones though, too.

Today's drones are the result of miniaturized electronics and batteries that themselves are advances in technology never seen before. With these advances begins the age of what is becoming known as, "electric aviation." Using electric motors to produce propulsion, these little flying machines can be built as helicopters small enough to fit in the palm of your hand, or airplanes with wingspans longer than that of an eagle.

As a long-time commercial pilot I hate to say it, but manned aircraft are quickly losing way to drones. Drones cannot only do what manned aircraft can do, drones can do what no manned aircraft can do. As of this moment there are thousands more drone pilots in the United States than pilots of manned aircraft. At the beginning of the year this book was written it was estimated that over a million drones have been sold.

The number of drones out there and the businesses they are creating are exploding. In part this is because of a factor that is very important to you and your customers. Drones don't cost much money to buy or operate. Even the pricier drones cost a fraction of what a manned aircraft costs that is used to do similar jobs. Drones don't cost much to operate because they don't carry hundreds of pounds of payload, and they don't have engines that run on flammable fuel. They have motors that run on batteries.

Drones don't need an airport, or even a hangar. Drones don't need a tow tractor or even wheels to move from place to place. You can just pick them up and walk away with sUAS drones. Manned aircraft often cost a fortune to maintain. Qualified airframe and power plant mechanics are required to maintain manned aircraft. Neither the machines nor their mechanics come cheap. Specialized tools and the parts for an airplane or helicopter are often as big an investment as the aircraft itself. On the other hand, repair of a drone can be accomplished by anyone. Spare parts for a drone can be purchased with pocket change. Tools to repair them can usually be found in any variety store.

Speaking as a commercial pilot, drones are usually more safe and suitable for operating over or around people or property than are manned aircraft. Flying a drone doesn't risk the life and limb of its crew. Neither does a drone put the people below it at risk. Making a video of your daughter's outdoor wedding for example, is much better done with a drone. You'll get unique views from eye level to sky level, have sharp video and photographs and your wedding guests probably won't even know the drone is there. You'll also pay a fraction of the cost of a manned aircraft for the services provided by a drone.

WHAT KIND OF BUSINESS CAN I DO WITH A DRONE?

Well, I've already pointed out a couple places drone businesses work. And without exaggerating, drones can do just about any aerial job you can imagine. Currently, drones are being used most for photography. Although you may have detected that drones are being used in the movies and commercials you see, the bulk of drone-based photography is being done in the real estate market. That is exactly why I decided to start my drone business as a real estate photography business.

...A GREAT WAY TO BECOME SUCCESSFUL IN A BUSINESS IS TO COPY THE WAY A SUCCESSFUL BUSINESS IS ALREADY WORKING.

It may sound like a bad idea to start a new business within the most popular area in a field. But I learned earlier in my life that a great way to become successful in a business is to copy the way a successful business is already working. That is one reason I chose real estate photography to start my new drone-based business. I figured there would be plenty of real estate drone operators. I could find out how they did business and establish my own business from clients they couldn't reach. But my plan didn't work. There were a lot fewer businesses to copy than I thought there would be. In fact, I couldn't even find a drone-based real estate business anywhere nearby my home. The reason was, all civilian drone-based businesses are brand new. There are few of them in the nation let alone in Burnet County, Texas where I live. That was exciting news for me and it should be for you, too. The drone market is wide open nationwide!

THE *FASTEST GROWING* DRONE-BASED BUSINESS IS IN THE AGRICULTURE INDUSTRY.

In order to test the market I was entering I put up my website, **http://beelinedrones.com**. I was astounded. My website was immediately overwhelmed with business. In the first twelve hours I got far more calls for work than I could have handled with a dozen drones. I could have kept drone crews busy full time. If that's a problem, it's a problem with which I am still dealing. And you will, too. I can't hire drone crews fast enough. I am convinced that using the principles and steps I learned and outlined in this book, you will find yourself with too many customers, too much business but a strategy for meeting customer demands just the same.

Real estate photography is in the number one slot for commercial use of drones. The second biggest user of drones will soon blow right past it. The *fastest growing* drone-based business is in the agriculture industry. Agricultural drone companies are already multiplying at breakneck speed. Each of them is busy hiring people to do jobs that did not even exist last year. They are even hiring people for jobs that do not currently exist, knowing that new agricultural jobs are being created with every new application discovered for them. Technology is being developed to meet each of these demands in unique ways. And each new application, each new drone built to meet it, requires people to handle the details. Marketing, manufacturing, modifying drones to meet customer demands, flying, instructing, servicing and selling these drones are all facets of the exploding job fields in the agricultural drone market. You and your new business could well be there among all that.

You shouldn't be intimidated that farmers are buying their own drones just to save time and money on their own farms. They can find and inspect livestock, do livestock or wild game counts, check fence and water lines, out buildings, farm roads and surrounding roads and gates that access their property. Walking and driving around the farm "for a look," is something I've spent hours doing on my own farm. Now other farmers and I can reduce those hours walking fence lines to minutes by using a drone. But this personal use of drones by farmers is small compared to more sophisticated agricultural uses farmers can't or don't want to do for themselves.

Professionally operated agricultural drones are being used to increase crop yield. The first story I heard about the capabilities of drones in this regard came from a professional now working exclusively with agricultural drones. At a recent convention for drone operators this specialist accompanied a presentation on the topic with pictures. The pictures had been taken regularly and progressively from a drone as the farmer/client grew a large field of wheat. The client acted on information derived from the pictures and advice from the specialist. Examining the data the drones gathered, specific parts of the same field were watered more in some places, less in others. In some cases drones were used to apply chemicals and fertilizer, but only at local spots that needed them. That task could have been done with drones, but I didn't hear if it had been done that way in this case. Certainly no traditional crop dusters were used. The farmer never sprayed the whole field with anything. The results of using the data supplied by drones on that field couldn't be argued with. The wheat field's yield increased by 1,000% from the preceding year! Clearly, drones belong in agriculture.

ACCORDING TO THE US BUREAU OF LABOR AND STATISTICS ONE OF THE MOST DANGEROUS JOBS IS WORKING AS A CROP DUSTER PILOT.

Companies are quickly appearing to build drones to meet specific agricultural needs. They are revolutionizing the conduct of crop dusting – the application of fertilizer, herbicide, insecticide and even seed by air. And here again is a place where drones should soon supersede manned aircraft doing the same job. According to the US Bureau of Labor and Statistics one of the most dangerous jobs is working as a crop duster pilot. Besides being routinely exposed to dangerous chemicals, crop duster pilots risk their lives in expensive aircraft flying at low level and high speed to deliver their loads. They even do it at night. Yikes! With a manned crop duster, a well sprayed field is one where the same amount of applicant drops evenly over the whole field. But not all fields need the same amount of an applicant on every square foot. Consequently, farmers are buying and applying tons of applicants that are unneeded, unwanted and even damage some of their crops in favor of others. Sometimes applying these applicants results in "overspray." In those cases, chemicals can end up drifting over fields that could be damaged by the applicant. Overspray can end up in watercourses, ponds and stock tanks, polluting them. It can also drift over machinery, occupied and otherwise. Overspray drifting over people can poison them. Drifting over yards and homes overspray can not only do damage to property.

Powerlines, windmills, antennas and guy wires pose a hazard to airplanes and helicopters dusting fields. Manned crop dusters too frequently hit them causing a fatal crash. Avoiding these obstructions cause crop dusters to leave areas near these obstructions unsprayed. Even when properly sprayed by manned dusters though, spray doesn't always reach under and along tree lines. Agricultural drones already address these problems. Drones can fly under wires, close by fences and tree lines, avoid streams and other water sources – or even apply chemicals directly to a water source without spraying the banks. Drones use far less applicant than a manned crop duster because they put just the right amount of applicant right where it is needed. If they overspray, they don't contain enough applicant to cause much of a hazard to people, damage to crops, machinery or other property.

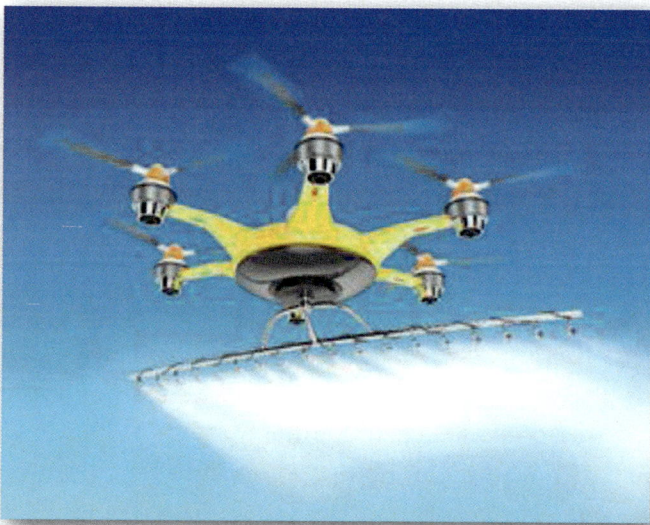

Like most drones, agricultural drones can be computer controlled and programmed to fly a route and spray pattern. In doing so they can individually treat certain areas and ignore others. They can fly individually or collectively at desired patterns and pre-programmed altitudes and speeds. Unlike manned crop dusters, drones can spray applicant irrespective of the wind direction, or in order to take advantage of the wind to better lay the applicant. Unlike airplanes, when drones fly at very low levels they can fly at speeds that won't damage the crops. And they can fly as low as necessary to get the right amount of applicant right where it needs to be without risking a pilot's life.

PEOPLE WANT VISUAL MEDIA...

The largest single commercial drone application across the board, even in real estate and agriculture, is in producing photographs and video. People want visual media of virtually anything that focuses their interest. Whether it is shots of chemical drums inside a vast warehouse or a close-up view of a hail damaged roof, drones can fit the bill. Movies and commercials are already opting out of using manned aircraft to do their video work in favor of drones. News stations are using drones instead of expensive and often less responsive manned aircraft. Drones can also be used in engineering inspections of roads and bridges, powerlines and supporting structures, windmill generators and tall towers like those used to transmit microwave and cell phone signals. Foresters can examine trees for insect infestations, plan fire trails or check existing ones, plan or observe timber cutting operations while checking erosion prevention efforts where the trees are felled. Fish hatcheries can track underwater migrations, count fry, check water temperatures and even track tagged fish. Two and three dimensional cameras mounted on drones are already used to aid and track the progress of open pit mining operations.

OIL, GAS AND CHEMICAL REFINERIES OFFER MORE OPPORTUNITIES TO USE DRONES.

The oil and gas industry is rife with applications for drones. Possibly seeing a downturn in the need for helicopters, a major offshore oil field helicopter company has just made a major investment in providing drones for their customers. They found out that they can inspect offshore oil and gas production platforms in two days with a drone that formerly took seventeen days landing crews on the rigs with helicopters. Oil, gas and chemical refineries offer more opportunities to use drones. Inspecting areas containing hazardous chemicals, high rise structures like flame towers and cracking towers, and following pipes to check their continuity and condition all offer opportunities for using drones. Oil production field managers can check equipment condition and function, track production efforts, equipment or well malfunctions and detect spills and their extent.

Using specialized cameras and lenses expands the regime in which photographic drones are being used in these plants, and other places. Thermal cameras for example, can tell when a pipe is hot or not. Thermal and specialized lenses can see a pipe joint leaking something invisible to the visual spectrum. Other drones already carry "sniffers" to detect gas leaks or the presence of chemicals and poisonous gasses like hydrogen sulfide (H2S), a common threat to refinery or oil platform workers.

Which brings up another use of drones. They *should* be used whenever human life or limb is at risk. Industrial accident sites, train wrecks, hazardous material spills and mass casualty incidents all call out for the use of drones. Police and emergency responders can by remote observation better and more safely allocate an effective response with people and equipment. Drone-based coverage also offers video recording of these events for future assessment, determining an accident's cause, to conduct investigations and to produce video material for training purposes.

DRONES CAN AND SHOULD BE USED WHEREVER FALLS ARE A RISK.

Anytime a ladder is employed a drone can probably go up to observe rather than sending a person where they can be injured in a fall. Drones have already made it unnecessary for building inspectors and insurance adjusters to walk on a steep roof, such as conducting close-up inspections of a new roof or to look for damage after a storm.

Instead of climbing any towers or high structure for routine inspections, do it with a drone. The inspection can be completed while the pilot and inspector stand on the ground nearby. Or the pilot can capture the information and send it live or in a computer file from the site to an engineer's office somewhere. My drone company has some recent experience inspecting windmill generators in West Texas. We can inspect the windmill tower, of course. But we can also make close up examination of the blades, a process which takes many hours putting the inspector at risk dangling from a rope and harness. Inspecting the blades and towers with a drone also keeps the generator out of service for a much shorter time. Inspecting these towers taught us the lesson of archiving. Regardless of what you are doing with your drones, archived data sells just as well the second and third time your customer needs it as it did the first time. Terabytes of such data can be kept on the camera chips, your company servers or stored at remote locations for very little money nowadays.

Cameras commonly used on even low priced drones often have previously unheard of capability and video quality. They provide ultra-high zoom and un-pixilated resolution. Even distant objects show up without distortion. As noted earlier, they can stop action and produce clear and crisp imagery of even swift moving objects. They can also speed up the action. Gyroscopes operating camera gimbals are now considered the norm when you purchase a baseline camera drone. These provide a stable platform for your camera that dampens out virtually all the vibration that can be caused by maneuvering the drone or encountering turbulence. Many drones come with camera mounts that allow the camera and gimbal mount to operate while disconnected from the drone. Shots taken from the ground and those taken from a drone can often augment each other this way.

"ON-DEMAND SERVICE" COULD ALSO MEAN YOU WILL PUSH A BUTTON AND GET A DRONE TO RESPOND.

"On demand" services by drones are on the forefront of new drone-based applications. If someone needs something delivered, it will soon be done by a drone. Several package delivery services are currently evaluating and validating drone-based delivery service. *When* – not *if* - it happens you may well have the package of coffee you ordered dropped on your doorstep by a drone. Likewise, that critical part required to keep your production line moving may not stop at the factory door but be dropped off on the production line by a drone before returning to its base. "On-demand service" could also mean you will push a button and get a drone to respond. Push a button in a community park and your order from a distant restaurant could deliver a hamburger by drone to your picnic table.

Push another button and a drone could deliver a defibrillator to people rendering aid to someone having a heart attack. Another button could put the 9-1-1 operator on alert and deliver a video link to pass to the emergency service en route to the location. Drones have already been used by search and rescue crews to find lost people. A company is experimenting with using multiple drones that can be dispatched for coordinated searches over a wide area. Should the search area be remote, individual drones can be linked to another single overhead command drone platform. These would pass video links to a central search and rescue coordination center.

Drones can deliver survival supplies to a lost hiker. Drones can drop fire extinguishing agent on a fire, or a life ring to a drowning person falling from a dock, a boat in the middle of a lake or person fallen overboard from a ship at sea.

Anywhere a security camera is now mounted a drone could perch for continuous observation and if necessary, immediate dispatch. High security areas such as airports, casinos, schools and industrial complexes are places where drone patrols can be used. Drones carrying motion detectors and infrared cameras can do the work of a "cop on the beat," protecting people who walk alone at night, or to patrol for and spot intruders at homes and businesses. Fire fighters will use drones with infrared cameras to see hotspots in a smoky fire or to locate stranded people inside or on top of a burning building.

So you ask what you can do with a drone. Do you see that tsunami of opportunity coming yet? You should be getting excited! Maybe this chapter has inspired you to move forward with a business in some other application no one has heard of yet. If so, read on and see how to start your business. Your next step should be to focus on the facet of the industry you want to work in. You should see this new business you start as both a commitment to, and a foothold in the implementation of drone technology. In coming chapters you'll see how to plan for your business to grow and spread into places you can't imagine right now. You can expect that customers will bring you new and interesting ideas for using drones to support them. Whether a friend asks you to film his lake party, or the county sheriff asks you to work with law enforcement officers to look for a lost Alzheimer's patient – your drone business is going to grow into something more than the business you start.

SO WHAT DRONE BUSINESS SHOULD I START?

Whatever business you do, start with and focus on one business and dig into it. When you set your sights on a new business, pick *one* business or job you *want* to do. Don't pick twenty-seven businesses you *could* do, or pick even one you won't like.

PICKING *ONE* BUSINESS WILL ALLOW YOU TO FOCUS YOUR EFFORTS ON ITS SUCCESS.

Otherwise you'll dilute your energy and expend your assets chasing down opportunities instead of developing them. You might well spend yourself out of assets, energy and business without having seized any of those opportunities you could have developed if you focused on just one. And work on one job you *want* to do that will make you happy. It is easier to get passionate about something you love to do. Starting a new business is challenging. Enjoying your job keeps you motivated when you might otherwise get discouraged.

In picking your drone business, remember. "If you can imagine it, you can do it." This is your day in the sun, a time to break out from "normal." You have a chance to start over in something entirely new. Look to people you love and trust to help you focus on a job you'll love doing. Look to people doing magnificent things right now with drones for inspiration. Billionaire entrepreneur Mark Zuckerberg, is one such example.

He is currently very much into building drone businesses. One of his concepts that already has wings is a solar powered drone designed to fly in the high upper atmosphere. Flying far above commercial air traffic, it is designed to stay aloft for weeks or months at a time. These high altitude drones will transmit internet signals where no infrastructure for the internet currently exists.

Mr. Zuckerberg has an internet company you may have heard about. It's called "Facebook." Do you suspect his drone business might just help his internet business? Take your inspiration from others. Maybe your first drone-based business can promote your second…and third…and so on.

Before you start buying anything - plan. Do your homework. Find out all you can about the business you want to do. You might actually find someone doing what you plan to do. You might find someone with a large market doing something that can be done better with a drone. If so, learn from those who do that job well. See how they do it and copy their success. Surf the web for companies involved in some facet of that business with drones. See what they are doing and how they are doing it.

When you find a job you want your new company to do, do more and focused research about it. Use web searches for information. Read blogs. They are often full of great ideas. The web will point out more business leads. Look them up and follow them for ideas and information on doing your business. As your ideas and objectives become more solid, focus your search for information. Don't just hide behind your computer screen, either. Whenever possible work face-to-face with people involved in drones.

One organization that can help you is probably right in your neighborhood. The American Academy of Model Aeronautics www.modelaircraft.org is an organization of passionate pilots of remote controlled aircraft. We used to call their aircraft, "radio controlled model aircraft." Make no mistake. These are drones flown for recreational purposes. Among the great advantage of being a member of an AMA group, you'll meet people who have the expertise, skill and patience to help you become proficient at flying remote controlled aircraft – including your drone. Allow yourself to become infected with their enthusiasm. Listen to their ideas and advice. And as part of the AMA, learn more about flying and employing the capabilities of your drones. Conventions are also an infectious environment for people looking for inspiration on starting a drone-based business.

YOU WILL COME AWAY FROM A CONVENTION WITH FAR MORE THAN WHAT YOU SPEND TO ATTEND.

You can find where they are taking place by typing, "drone conventions" into an internet search engine. Drone conventions often go on for days, usually in nice hotels located in fun places. One of the best is *InterDrone,* The International Drone Conference and Exposition. Past events have been held in Las Vegas. If you are interested in drones, you will leave that convention with your enthusiasm on fire. There and at other conventions you will be exposed to more ideas and more technology than you can take in. Invest in yourself. Sign up for the whole convention. Attend talks by people who are in the business. Talk to vendors selling technology and ideas. Meet people who are ahead of you in the business. Spend time in conversation that will lead to ideas and inspiration. You will come away from a convention with far more than what you spend to attend. You will find ways to do your business that have already been proven to work. You will more than likely leave with contacts and associations with people with whom you will stay in touch for the rest of your career.

Get to know those around your town, county and state who fly drones. Like you, they should advertise on the web. Look for their sites. Even potential competitors are often willing to give you good advice. Meet the airport operators, the air traffic control personnel, and the people in the FAA Flight Standards District Office near where you live. Let them know what you are doing. Offer your cooperation and your service. Ask how you can help them. Perhaps you could participate in their safety programs and the FAA Safety Team (FAAST). And ask for their advice. These are all professional associations you can seek out that can do a great deal in contributing to your drone-based business operation becoming safe, legal, profitable, professional – and fun!

Don't re-invent what can be copied. Take what works and form it to meet your needs. Copy good ideas exactly, or improve upon them if it improves your business. Then when you have your objectives set and homework done, follow the steps outlined in this book for starting your own drone-based business.

WHO CAN START A DRONE BUSINESS?

Anyone with the imagination, will, savvy and ability to start any business should be able to start a business with drones. Drones are aircraft. They operate in the National Airspace System (NAS). They are under the regulation of the Federal Aviation Administration. FAA certificated pilots are required to fly them for commercial purposes. But there has been a change. Now those pilots don't have to be able to fly anything but drones. If you aren't a pilot or you are new to aviation, a knowledge of aviation is required to operate a business with drones. But don't be discouraged. You don't have to be a pilot to run a drone business. You can learn about flying where everyone learns about flying. Hire a flight instructor. Even if you don't intend to fly, you need to know about weather, airspace and other subjects that a flight instructor can teach you. The more you know about aviation, the better you can conduct your business. But keep in mind that people with vast and detailed aeronautical knowledge can be hired. I doubt any of the people who head the world's airlines are airline pilots. If that is true of the airlines, it should certainly apply to someone who wants to own and manage a drone business.

YOU'LL LEARN THE BASICS YOUR COMPANY'S PILOTS ARE DEALING WITH WHEN THEY FLY YOUR DRONES.

Many of the people involved in drone businesses are pilots, are drone pilots or become pilots and drone pilots. Often it was their fascination with flying or flying drones in particular that got them to start businesses with them. If you want to learn to fly a drone in order to better manage your business, I would encourage you to pursue that. Drone pilots flying for recreation do not require a pilot certificate or any medical certification. Go to a hobby shop or find drones for sale. Buy one you can fly indoors. You can find them for less than $20 that are no bigger than the palm of your hand. Start with short hops from the kitchen to the dining room table. Then get a bigger one you can fly outside and have some fun in the back yard chasing the cat. You'll learn the basics your company's pilots are dealing with when they fly your drones. When you get good enough with the toys, fly your own commercial drones for recreation.

THE RULES HAVE CHANGED

You may have heard that if you're going to fly a drone commercially you will need an FAA pilot certificate (pilot license). Not only would you have to possess a pilot certificate, you'd also need to remain current in what you fly.

Well, all that has changed, and changed for the better.

On June 21, 2016 the FAA published and released the, "Small Unmanned Aircraft Rule," also called 14 CFR, Part 107 or just, "Part 107" for short. Immediately prior to its release the FAA had a rather complicated and exclusive rule for operating commercial drones. Commercial drone operators were required to apply for what was known as a "333 exemption." If like me you possess one of these exemptions you are free to continue to operate under it until it reaches its two year expiration date. If on the other hand you are just about to start a commercial drone operation with small drones, Part 107 is for you. At least it is for you if you operate a drone weighing less than 55 pounds, at less than 100 miles per hour, at or below four hundred feet above the ground, under visual conditions in daylight. If on the other hand you plan to operate a large drone, plan to fly above 400 feet, faster than 100 miles per hour or fly on instruments you still need the 333 exemption. Your pilots will also require a private pilot's license at least. Flying a drone under instrument flight rules (IFR) requires an instrument rating as well.

Part 107 is designed for the commercial operator who plans to conduct business while flying "low and slow." (Less than 400 feet and less than 100 mph.) For that, the drone pilot will need the new pilot certificate called the "remote pilot airman certificate with a small UAS rating." More on the specifics of operating under Part 107 comes later in this book.

WHAT DOES IT COST TO START A DRONE BUSINESS?

Some of the answer to this question lies in what you plan to do with your drone. Let's look at an odd scenario I heard about from someone who insures drone operations. One of his potential clients didn't want to tell the insurance man why he wanted coverage on his drones. The insurance man drilled down though and found out that the potential client wanted to use his drones to fly inside the caldera of a volcano. He planned to photograph the lava at close range. He actually planned to fly there until his drone finally burned up. The potential client wanted insurance to replace his drone after he sacrificed it to the volcano. So what do you plan to do with your drone? If you plan to sacrifice it flying into volcanos, that's fine. Just plan for it. You can expect high equipment costs, but low insurance costs because nobody will insure an operation like that.

BUILD YOUR BUSINESS YOURSELF.

Your expenses in starting and running a drone-based company will largely be based on how you intend to use your drone. The best way to cut costs in starting your company is to do as much of the setup as possible by yourself. This is not so hard to do for a conventional drone business such as for photography. Set up a corporate entity, bank account, insurance and company bond. Do your own website and marketing. Familiarize yourself with the requirements of Part 107. Buy a drone and peripherals. For a one drone operation that will all cost you less than five thousand dollars. That number includes two drones because a one drone operation will stop when your only drone fails. Depending on how much outside help you pay for though, that five thousand dollar number can easily triple.

Bottom line: Build your business yourself. Don't worry. You can do this.

WHAT KIND OF DRONE DO I NEED?

If you have been thinking about starting a business with drones, you may already have spent time looking at them on the internet. There are hundreds of models of drones out there. There are an equal number of manufacturer's websites to tell you about them. And there are thousands of internet videos with any information you could want about any drone available. It may be backwards logic, but I have found that if you haven't decided what you want to do with a drone, shopping for them can give you some ideas. It's rather like picking up a tool and deciding what you can do with it. But if it works to get you excited and get your creative juices flowing, sit down and watch drone videos. You can also do it the traditional way and find the job you want to do, then choose the tool to do it.

As mentioned before, there are two categories of drones from which to choose: fixed wing (like an airplane) and rotary wing (like a helicopter).

Courtesy, 'Hoot' Gibson, Aerial ROW

Fixed wing drones are best for covering larger distances or doing a big job quickly. If you need a "big picture" looking at a large piece of real estate for instance, a fixed wing drone might be your choice. Flying along the length of river or across a wide valley doing a game study might be better served with a fixed wing drone, too. Fixed wing drones fly like an airplane. All drones are limited to a speed of one hundred miles per hour. Some fixed wing drones can do that. You can cover a lot of territory at that speed. Fixed wing drones don't always look like a conventional airplane. Some very capable and effective ones are quite small. They often look like little toy airplanes. Others are shaped like a dart. Your operation may use a fixed wing drone to augment what you do with the other type of drone.

Rotary wing drones can be used like fixed wing drones. They don't usually fly as fast as fixed wing drones but they can still cover a pretty wide area. At higher altitudes their camera can take in a wide swath of real estate. But rotary wing drones are best for getting slow and low. If you need pictures from a single point in space, if you're making close up video, flying in confined spaces like inside a warehouse or between trees and powerlines, rotary wing drones are the way to go. Since rotary wing drones can hover, they would be your choice for close up inspections of structures, or to climb up alongside a tall tower or take a detailed survey of a building or other structure. "Quad copters" are popular for photography. They're helicopters with multiple (four in this case) rotor systems. There are also rotary wing drones with two, six, or more rotors. Larger "multi-copters" are often used to carry more weight.

A drone is a tool, and with any tool you use the one best suited to the purpose. You may find that you will have a number of different drones of different categories and types to accommodate your jobs. Drones are both "general-purpose" and "purpose built." If you want to use your drone for multiple purposes or you expect to get employment in ways you can't anticipate at the moment, the general-purpose drone is for you. They usually come pre-assembled and have all the peripheral supports with them like controllers, batteries, chargers and spare parts. If you plan on doing just one function, like spraying liquid fertilizer on a golf course, you may want a purpose-built drone. Drone manufacturers are starting businesses focused on custom or purpose-built drones. The manufacturer will probably be the supplier of all your peripherals and spare parts. They may even provide training, supervision or continuing service after the sale.

SUMMARY: DECIDE WHAT YOU WANT TO DO AND FIGURE OUT HOW TO DO IT.

Once you decide what you want to do, you need to figure out what the best tool is to do the job. That's the kind of drone you need.

HOW MUCH WILL A DRONE COST?

Shop for the drone that will do the job. Then you'll have to choose the features you want. You can get a toy drone in a hobby shop to practice with for $12. Add a few batteries, some extra propellers to repair damaged ones and a multi-battery charger and the price doubles. It's the same way all the way up into the expensive drones. The more support equipment and spares you have, the higher your costs will be. A first generic commercial camera drone, in a case with all the peripherals and a couple batteries will cost between $1000 and $2000. Add spare parts, a half dozen drone batteries and a charger that handles them all and a stock of the other batteries the camera and controller use and you can add another $1000 or so to the ticket. But you're not done.

As I mentioned earlier, if you're going to start out as a one drone operation you'll need two drones. If you only have one drone, Murphy's Law (Anything that can go wrong will go wrong) says your one drone will break when you need it. The same advice goes for your controller and any peripherals, like your camera. I recommend that you start with two complete drone kits that include a drone and the desired peripherals like a camera and a controller. I buy my drones in hard cases that are made for them. You might decide to save money there and buy your own cases and modify them to fit your drone. But your drones should live in cases if you want that investment (and consequently your business) protected whether you store your drone or move it around to job sites.

Since you will most probably be the repair and service center for the drones you fly, you will need spare parts. If you fly a copter you'll certainly need another full set of rotors (propellers). Since some rotors on multi-copters spin clockwise and others spin counterclockwise you have to buy them in sets. Fixed wing drones should have spare propellers as well. Ask the manufacturer or a supply house what spares they recommend that you keep on hand for your operation. While you have them on the phone, ask what they recommend to get you back in the air if you have a major problem or a crash. Manufacturers often service what they sell. You can also do the work yourself. A motor replacement or replacement of a structural member is not routine, but you can keep the parts on hand to accommodate such things. You can buy all the parts that compose your drone, including the major structural members of the drone. In time you may have a collection of such parts, but you don't need them all at the outset. If you need a part you don't have, you can usually get parts for the most common drones in a couple days from the parts houses and manufacturers.

LET'S TALK ABOUT THE MOST EXPENSIVE PART OF YOUR OPERATION...BATTERIES.

This is the dawn of the "age of electric aviation." If you're out of electricity, you're out of business. Drones use lots of battery power. Your drone may be expensive, but once you buy it you're done with that investment. Not so with batteries. A significant chunk of your startup budget will consist of stocking enough batteries to get started. Then the biggest expense over the long run of a drone-based business will be keeping your drone(s) in batteries. So let's address those.

Make sure you buy plenty of each kind your drone needs. Build a budget that devotes a certain percentage of your profit to keep feeding your business with batteries. Regardless of which batteries you use, buy rechargeable batteries. As a commercial drone operator you'll get your money's worth out of them. Keep lots of them charged and ready, too. Recharge them when they discharge so you always have a ready supply. The drone, its peripherals (like cameras) and the controller all use batteries. Unfortunately your drone, its controller and the camera or peripherals probably all use *different* batteries. Some drones can be modified to power the peripherals with the same type of battery the drone motors use.

You'll need to become an expert with batteries. Different batteries charge differently. That means you'll need different chargers. Batteries that drive one drone are more often not compatible with other drones. So you'll have to become expert at buying the right batteries, storing, recharging and carrying spare batteries. You'll also have to learn where to get the best prices and quality in your batteries.

"Lithium Polymer" or "LiPo" batteries in particular are going to be big items in your budget. They are the heart of the drone. They are really modern miracles. They are unlike any battery made before. As much as anything else, these batteries are responsible for opening up these unique business opportunities to us. They are powerful enough to drive a drone's propulsion motors and create enough lift to carry their own weight as well as the drones'. They deliver 100% of their substantial power as soon as it is needed. But most important, they are the lightest battery ever made for the power they provide.

"LiPo's" deliver their power steadily until they are exhausted. One of their limitations is that they can only deliver that power to the average sUAS for 20 to 30 minutes at a time. Another limitation is that they cost about $100 a piece. At that price, you can see that having enough LiPo batteries for a day of flying will cost you. They're rather touchy and exotic, too. 'Exotic' means they have a tendency to catch fire and explode when improperly handled. Storing LiPo's means more than just putting boxes of them in the refrigerator. Volumes of information and advice fills the internet regarding how to store and get the most life out of a LiPo battery. No one seems to agree on how much life that is. Most experts do agree however, that LiPo's do not react well to physical damage. Transporting and handling them takes some special planning and care to prevent damage. They need to be kept in special storage, carried in special explosion proof carriers and charged carefully in order to get the most life from them. Limitations aside, without LiPo's the "age of electric aviation" would be a myth.

Information on battery management, storage, handling, charging and how batteries are constructed fills manufacturers' web sites, internet blogs and drone advice columns. As your expertise grows with them you'll learn the tricks to get the most out of them. But here's one of those tricks you should learn. Find out how to modify your drone to run the camera off one LiPo battery, while a second LiPo powers the drone. And another pointer: while you are shopping for a drone, pay attention to how the batteries are connected. A guide would be that, "simple is good." Some batteries are simple. They plug right into the drone's body. But electrical systems on other drones are frankly nightmares. They are fragile nests of tiny wires susceptible to damage. Their batteries likewise have tiny, flimsy plugs and exposed wires that do not lend well to long life. These batteries probably won't fail before their connectors do because the connectors are the weak link in the system. One drone manufacturer requires an expensive attachment built into each LiPo battery rather than into the drone itself. As a result you'll spend about forty percent more for batteries for this model of drone. When you're shopping for drones, pay attention to the batteries, their construction and their costs.

You'll also soon find that battery chargers are important to understand when you buy your drone. The charger that may come with your drone will usually not be large enough to charge the number of batteries you will need for a commercial job. As with batteries for your drone, chargers can be bought on the internet or in hobby stores. When you buy a larger or more capable charger not offered by the drone manufacturer, you take some risk. Some drone batteries won't charge on these chargers. Usually the batteries with specialized adapters particular for one kind of drone don't work on off brand chargers. Check to make sure your batteries fit before you buy an off brand charger. You'll also need to learn how to "balance" the charge on your batteries. Hints on doing that are out there on the web, but they also come with the instruction guide found with most charging kits.

HERE'S WHY YOU BOUGHT THE BOOK.

If you just rip this page out of this book and hopefully return it to the shelf before the store manager sees you, you'll have the outline for starting a business with drones.

These are the steps to starting a business so you can **Make Money With Drones**:

1. Figure out what you want to do as a business using drones.
2. Obtain a corporate entity.
3. Comply with Part 107 or obtain an FAA "333 exemption."
4. Learn and comply with the regulations.
5. Learn how to fly a drone, or find someone to fly it for you.
6. Buy a drone that will do the work for your business.
7. Set up the business

That's it. Just do those things on the list and you should end up as a successful owner of a business flying drones that is safe, legal and profitable. But let me elaborate.

Chapter 1

FIGURE OUT WHAT YOU WANT TO DO AS A BUSINESS USING DRONES

There is a reason that I list this as step one in building a successful drone-based business. This is the step that will set the objective for your business. Lewis Carroll, author of <u>Alice in Wonderland</u> is usually given credit for saying, "If you don't know where you are going, any road will get you there." Whether he said it or not, it is true where starting a business is concerned. And so it is with your drone business. As recommended in the first chapters, pick a drone application you will *enjoy*. Then, focus on making it into a business. The prologue and the pages that got you to this point should have given you plenty of food for thought about what you can do - for and with - a drone related business. Now it's time to settle in on exactly what drone business you want to pursue.

YOU ARE ABOUT TO START ON A LONG JOURNEY.

Once you pick a facet of the drone business that excites you, do your homework. Find out what it takes to reach your objective. Before you get too far into your investigation, make sure you can make a profit doing the business. Find out if and how others have done the job before you. Then, if you can do the business and make an acceptable profit, write a business plan. I can feel a number of you cringe when reading that last line. Sorry. From my experience and perspective you need an objective and a plan to reach it. You need to have it in writing. I didn't say carve it in stone. A business plan is a living document. It will change as your business changes. You are writing it in order to read it. It will keep you on track as long as you refer to it often. When your goals change, change the plan to focus on reaching those new goals. Your bank, your lawyer, your accountant and probably your employees should be familiar with it, or at least the broad objectives outlined in it. They can all support you better when they know where you are going.

You are about to start on a long journey. Without a business plan you fall into the group Lewis Carroll was talking about. You're drifting. When you start off on a long journey you don't just jump in your car without knowing where you are going. You look at a road map. You refer to it as your trip continues. That road map is your business plan. It shows where you were, where you are and where you're trying to reach. With drones in particular a road map is important because you're making a trip into virgin territory. No one has been there before. The only map you have may be the one you produce. So take the time to make your own map. Write and update your business plan.

Chapter 2

OBTAIN A CORPORATE ENTITY

A corporate entity is designed to protect your assets.
Let's put aside the discussion of what corporate entity to use for your business for a minute. If you plan to file for a 333 exemption you *must* have a corporate structure of some kind in order to file. The FAA does not care which particular corporate structure you use to run that business. But even if you plan to operate under Part 107, you'll need a corporate entity to protect your assets and identify yourself. A corporate entity divides your personal assets from the corporation, and from other businesses you may own. Whether you choose a sole proprietorship, partnership, corporation, a limited liability company or some other structure is up to you. Selecting the right structure for your business will take a little research. You can do that on your own on the internet at no cost. Only then might I suggest you seek some professional help (for which you will pay something). When you decide which corporate structure you want, getting a corporation started is not tough, expensive or something you can't do yourself. With a little research on the web and a couple telephone calls to your state's "secretary of state," you can create a corporate entity for yourself. Then, if you are operating under 333 exemption and not just under Part 107, you can note that corporate name on your FAA application for exemption.

Here is some advice to consider in actually becoming a corporate entity. You should select the kind of corporation that best matches the long term intent of your business. Consider which one offers the best protection of your assets. Consider also which one protects your heirs with a structure that will fit your business for as long as it stays in business, whether you're alive to run it or not. If you don't have a corporation yet, consider what you will name your company. "XYZ Drone Company" is not a particularly clever name, but it is an example of what you want your customers to realize. You are a drone company. Your company name may or may not include the corporate structure. For example, you may become "XYZ Drone Company, Inc." In the introductory letter on the first page of a 333 exemption request you will file under your corporate structure. For example:

> "XYZ Drone Company" is a Texas-based Limited Liability Partnership…"

Like me, maybe you already have a company in which you can run your drone business. Before my drone business came along I set up a Limited Liability Corporation (LLC). I did my homework and started a company to fit the kind of business I expected to do for the rest of my life, not for just one application. I used that company name on my FAA "333 exemption" request. But the company, "Eagle Training Solutions, LLC" didn't have a name that customers would recognize when looking for a drone operator. So I got a "dba," meaning "Doing Business As."

If you already have a company and want to add a dba, it's not difficult to arrange. In Texas where I live, getting a "dba" just took a visit to the county clerk's office at our local courthouse. After putting a signature on a page before a notary, a couple polite conversations and paying the county clerk fifteen dollars my company Eagle Training Solutions, LLC is *doing business as* "Beeline Drones." My LLC still has the corporate structure I do business within, but now a dba resides within that LLC. The dba, "Beeline Drones" portrays my company to people looking for a drone business, and allows me to identify my company to the FAA as a corporate entity for my application for exemption.

"Eagle Training Solutions, LLC is a Texas-based corporation doing-business-as "Beeline Drones."

The life of the dba in Texas is 10 years. Then I have to go back to the courthouse. If you already have a company under which you wish to do your drone business, a "dba" might suit you, too.

Whether or not you have a company, you might want to obtain a new corporation rather than a "dba." Your new company would not only bear the business name that suits your drone business. It would separate the assets and liability of your drone business from any other personal or business assets or entities you have. Besides satisfying the FAA with a corporate name for an exemption request, having a corporate entity will satisfy your bank, your customers and vendors and the IRS that you are incorporated.

An option to success in most business is to work with somebody else who already knows the business. That applies to drone businesses, too. One option is to work *for* somebody in the drone business. There are many new drone businesses opening up. Look for one of these companies to work with. Spend some time learning where the opportunities lie. Go to a drone convention. Bring a resume.

One area of employment in drones that is wide open is in companies looking for drone pilots. If you are already a certificated pilot, companies like mine are looking for you. (Send *me* a resume!) Whether you're an experienced pilot or not, if you want a job flying drones I suggest that you buy a drone and start flying it. Buy one you might use in your own business one day. Start logging your flights. Follow the steps outlined in this book for getting proficient with it. If you are a new or low time pilot, note that piloting drones is a flying job you can get even without much experience. Speaking for myself, I am much more likely to hire a less experienced pilot proficient with drones than a more experienced pilot who needs training to fly them.

Another option to success in the drone business is to work *with* someone else. There are several ways to work with other people in drone related businesses while you start and expand your own. These relationships can provide you with a business model, new opportunities, a source of assets, and information and assistance with your own drone operations. These associations also provide income. Among these working relationships with others are franchises, partnerships, corporations and informal and formal affiliations.

Franchises come from a company that will authorize you to conduct business in the same manner as the company from which you purchase it. People who buy a franchise do so because they expect a reasonable return on their investment. They're not looking for individuality or lots of latitude in how the business is conducted. In most franchises in fact, there's little or no latitude in how business is conducted. You – the franchisee - do business the company way. McDonald's restaurants are a great example of a franchise. No matter where in the world you go, a Big Mac is a Big Mac. If you own a McDonald's franchise you will make Big Macs the same way as every other McDonald's franchise. And that's okay. People like the way McDonald's makes their Big Mac. As a result, as a company McDonald's can virtually guarantee their franchisees a tremendous market. It's not a guarantee your business will be successful, but you can often make good money with a franchise.

Becoming a company that sells franchises might fit you, too. If you develop a product or process that is making big money for you, other people will notice. In that case, you might consider selling that product or process as a franchise. You may even be approached to offer that product or process to other business people to franchise for you.

If your business is doing well but you want to add another line to it, you may decide to purchase a franchise to add to your existing business. For example, you may like a model of drone you use. As your business grows you might decide to sell a drone and a line of training and peripherals. In that case you might buy a franchise with right to sell the drone and it parts. The drone manufacturer may issue you a license to sell their product and train others how to use it, which you can do in company with your host business.

Partnerships usually allow more latitude in the conduct of your business than a franchise. You and your partner(s) co-own the company. You and your partners will decide together how your business is conducted, how customers are found and how customer service is provided. Depending on how much of the partnership you own, you share the decisions and a percentage of the profits and the losses. Partnerships work best when the partners get along. Not getting along with your partners is a drawback of a partnership and a common reason cited when they don't work. Another drawback to a partnership is that you and your partners are each and severally liable. That means you and your partners can get each other sued, or driven into bankruptcy if things go wrong.

Keep in mind that depending on how you and someone else work a business together, you can end up in a partnership without even knowing it. Even with no document declaring you a partner, someone with whom you work can call you one. If they do that in court it's usually up to you to prove them wrong, a case of "guilty until proven innocent." I've seen this happen when some unsavory character wants to share his losses, or a lawsuit with a partner. That's a hard lesson lots of folks learn in a courtroom. If you are doing similar business with others it's a good idea to consult with your attorney, CPA or both about what constitutes a partnership. You only want to be in a partnership if you know you're entering into it willingly.

Corporations are often a wise choice for structuring your business in this litigious society. In a law suit, corporations offer its owner(s) a certain amount of protection of their personal and possibly their business assets. Corporations are also offered some tax advantages that other business structures do not enjoy. Corporations also exist in perpetuity. Your employees and heirs will appreciate the protection of a corporation if you are no longer around to run it for them. Get to know the differences between a C-Corp, S-Corp, a Limited Liability Partnership (LLP) or Limited Liability Corporation (LLC). All of them provide structures with certain advantages and disadvantages for conducting your business. This book is not focused on addressing these, but corporations are not complicated to understand or even difficult to set up. Do some homework and look up the pros and cons of various corporate structures. Put your intentions in writing in your business plan. Once you have a corporate structure in mind, share your business plan with your attorney and/or a CPA. Dog-ear the page about your corporate structure for them. When you've heard their advice, make your decision and then file the paperwork yourself. The more you learn about corporations, how they work and how to set one up before starting one, the less money you will have to pay for by the hour to learn from an attorney.

Informal Organizations between companies with similar interests can enable people and corporate entities to solve problems that cannot be solved by any single entity alone. That's a stuffy way of saying that getting together with another drone operator to complete a big job is a good way to get a job done that you can't do by yourself.

I AM WARY OF ANY BUSINESS DEAL I CAN'T "DO ON A HANDSHAKE."

Don't be afraid of informal business relationships. We all have informal relationships in everything we do. For example: we seek advice or assistance from a friend, an expert we've never met, or the owner of a business similar to our own – even our competitors. One of the nice things I like about informal organizations is that they frequently blossom into formal relationships. If you don't believe that, you've never been married.

Even with a large corporate structure and a formal contract in place I am wary of any business deal I can't "do on a handshake." Formal and informal agreements are struck on a supposition of trust between the parties involved. Without trust you have no business striking any kind of deal. Even if I expect to form a formal business relationship with someone, I like working informally at the outset. "Handshake deals" are generally uncomplicated. Informal affiliations do not limit those who participate in them. You get an idea about how the different parties work and how well they work together.

Even in informal agreements though, I always recommend writing a contract. The most important purpose of a contract is to remind the parties involved what was agreed to when the parties shook hands. I know people look at contracts as something that they can bring to court. But I have rarely found the need to hire a lawyer or talk to a judge about anything. When I sign a contract it happens after both parties reviewed the details. A contract may never be referred to again after it is signed. But if confusion develops about what was agreed to, a contract is a great memory jogger. Each party should be clear about an agreement before it is signed, and clear again if a contract needs to be brought out and read.

I must surely have written hundreds of contracts in my lifetime. Here's an example of one:

Gordon Shaub (Son) agrees to mow the Shaub residence front and back lawn on Saturday morning, (date), completing the job by noon of that day. If the job is completed by noon to the satisfaction of Patrick Shaub (Dad), Patrick Shaub will pay Gordon Shaub $25. If the job is not completed by noon to the satisfaction of Patrick Shaub, the efforts of Gordon

Shaub will be considered free gratis and the job completed by sunset to the satisfaction of Patrick Shaub.

You may think that this contract is both simple and unnecessary. If so, you have never tried to get a teenage son to mow the lawn on a Saturday. If it appears the son is about to default on the contract, Dad can remind his son, "The contract specifies 'by noon' or you don't get paid."

If either party needs to get specific about what constitutes a "satisfactory" job, or the definition of "noon" the contract can be extended. But with my sons and with people with whom I do business we don't split hairs. I keep my contracts simple. The best contract is one that ends with both parties agreeing that the items on it were completed as planned. Everybody leaves satisfied. By the way, that lawn mowing contract was the kind of exercise that helped teach my sons how contracts work. As a consequence, all three of my sons, now adults and fine businessmen, aren't afraid of any deal – formal or informal.

I have a number of affiliations with other drone operators. The first informal affiliation I struck for a job in the drone business was for a single project. I knew it was too big for me to handle. The project was to use a drone in an application that was new to me. I was also out of the country at the time the work was supposed to start. I called a friend to help. He too owned a drone business too small for the job. So we both struck an informal relationship with another drone operator who would fly his drone on the job to augment my friend's efforts. That covered the gap and satisfied the customer. This affiliation worked well. As a consequence I'm sure we'll have more opportunities to work together again, either on one of my projects or one of theirs.

"IF YOU WANT TO *GET*, YOU HAVE TO *GIVE*."

People always enjoy working with other people they already know and like. That's a strength in informal affiliations. My affiliates generally have common professional values as well as a common outlook on life in general. Most important, we trust each other. As a result, our affiliations generally produce a better product than one operator in the affiliation could do single handedly. These affiliations also open up opportunities with and between the affiliates later.

Here's a last word in favor of informal business affiliations. The most successful man I ever met also happens to be the wealthiest. About the time I was starting my first business he taught me a great lesson. He said that when he is asked by people how they can become as wealthy as he is, his response is always the same. He asks them, "What have you given?" When the mystified look comes over the questioner's face, my friend goes on. "If you want to *get*, you have to *give*." I follow his advice to this day. It has worked in my business relationships, my personal relationships and most especially in my marriage. My wife and I generally try to "out-give" each other. We've been happily married for forty years. I don't think that's a coincidence. My wealthy friend has been married as long as my wife and I have, too. He and I are on the same page here. When you spend more time focused on what you can give to a relationship than what you are going to get out of it, you almost always get far more than you give.

In summary: You need to create a corporate entity to protect your business and personal assets. A business entity also helps identify you to customers, the FAA and supporting elements of your business, like banks and insurance companies. Regardless of what entity you choose, form a contract with those with whom you do business. Work to give more than you get.

Chapter 3

COMPLY WITH PART 107 OR FILE FOR AND OBTAIN AN FAA 333 EXEMPTION

There's good news for small drone operators! The "Small Unmanned Aircraft Rule" is now law. You will find it in Part 14 of the Code of Federal Regulations (CFR) which is "Aeronautics and Space." So the rule is officially referred to as "14 CFR, Part 107," or just "Part 107." What all that bureaucratic detail boils down to is that now, people who want to start a business with small drones (sUAS) can do so with minimal hassle. If they're flying small drones (sUAS) less than 55 lbs., under four hundred feet AGL and they have the new "Remote Pilot with UAS Rating" certificate, they can operate under Part 107. They no longer need to apply for the complicated "333 exemption" and its accompanying Certificate of Authorization (COA) just to start a business with drones. Don't totally discount the "333 exemption," though. There is still a wide open place for one. Flying a large drone (over 55 lbs.), flying faster than one hundred miles per hour or flying IFR for example. We'll get to Part 107 in a minute. But because the "333" still has valid uses for drone operators we'll start there.

Previous to the introduction of Part 107 everyone who wanted to fly drones commercially had to request a "333 exemption." That is, they had to receive an exemption from certain Federal Aviation Regulations. This exemption was issued under section 333 of Public Law 112. So we call that exemption a "333 exemption." Writing my request took a good deal of work and a six month wait before I received it. Now I can do the business I originally proposed to do under a 333 by utilizing the much more simple and straight-forward Part 107 regulations. But that's okay. Now I have a "333." I can continue to operate under it until it expires. If I want to fly a drone that does not qualify for operating under Part 107, I can get a modified COA and operate under my "333 exemption."

Since I got my business started, I've received proposals to do work with a drone that weighs more than 55 pounds. That requires a 333. I can't do that under Part 107. I'm glad I have my 333. So let me tell you how to apply for a "333 exemption."

333 OPERATIONS

You have probably figured out by now that anyone operating a drone business will have to be thoroughly familiar with the rules and information available from the Federal Aviation Administration. The handiest portal for finding these rules is the government regulation website, **ecfr.gov**. There you will find the entire "Code of Federal regulations (CFR)." In browsing the site, look for "Title 14 – Aeronautics and Space." That part of the CFRs will take you to the Federal Aviation Regulations.

As a drone business operator you should also become accustomed to searching **faa.gov/uas.** There you will find by using the search block, "FAR 107." All the FAA has published about Part 107 will be available for you to read there. You will also find yourself backing into the home page **faa.gov** in the normal conduct of your business as a drone operator.

HOW TO OBTAIN A "333 EXEMPTION."

The **faa.gov** website explains the exemption from federal law that commercial drone operators must have if they do not qualify or do not want to operate under Part 107.

"By law, any aircraft operation in the national airspace requires a certificated and registered aircraft, a licensed pilot, and operational approval grants the Secretary of Transportation the authority to determine whether an airworthiness certificate is required for a UAS to operate safely in the National Airspace System (NAS). This authority is being leveraged to grant case-by-case authorization for certain unmanned aircraft to perform commercial operations prior to the finalization of the Small UAS Rule [Part 107], which will be the primary method for authorizing small UAS operations once it is complete. The Section 333 Exemption process provides operators who wish to pursue safe and legal entry into the NAS a competitive advantage in the UAS marketplace, thus discouraging illegal operations and improving safety. It is anticipated that this activity will result in significant economic benefits, and the FAA Administrator has identified this as a high priority project to address demand for civil operation of UAS for commercial purposes."

See FAA.gov/uas

Let me offer some observations based on what I learned in writing and obtaining my own 333 exemption request.

Done right, preparing your 333 exemption request is the most important step in the process of starting your drone-based business. Properly prepared it will get your business on track. Executed as written, your business will run smoothly and efficiently, as well as safely, legally and profitably. The process of writing an exemption request should be the most time consuming single element in starting your drone business. Your application will provide the bulk of the information you will put into your business plan and later, your company General Operating Manual. People have a natural urge to rush this application step – to get busy and get the business going. I encourage you to take a patient and disciplined look at the details of how you will conduct your business. Then write a business plan for yourself and your exemption request for the FAA. One should complement the other.

The less patient of us hire a consultant to do this work. Consultants promise fast filing of your 333 exemption request. Most guarantee some satisfaction - like a reduced fee - if your request isn't accepted. If hiring a consultant to write your 333 is your plan, take note. Consultants don't work cheap. Fees consultants commonly charge could double or triple the expense of starting your drone business. More importantly, in hiring a consultant you are counting on them to tell the FAA how you wish to conduct your business. Nobody knows your business plan like you do, certainly not a consultant who is focused on getting your exemption request filed before moving on to the next client. Your exemption request consequently may be written and submitted with whatever gets it approved quickly. The FAA promises to get the results of your request back within 120 days of its posting in the Federal Register, whether a consultant files it or you do. Based on your request – or the one filed in your name - if it is approved, your 333 exemption and a Certificate of Authorization (COA) will spell out exactly what you can do with a drone and how you can do it. If someone wrote your exemption for you, and your exemption and COA doesn't tell you that you can do something you wanted to do, then you'll have to apply for another COA. You can do that yourself, but if you use a consultant to "get it right" this time, you'll be out of pocket some more cash. When he's done, you'll still be out another 60 days after the new COA request is submitted. So you might as well do the whole thing yourself.

It takes time and considerable thought for a business owner to create a design for their business. After you have a business plan, writing your own exemption request will guide you through the confusion of starting up and running your business within the regulations. Although it is time consuming, writing a good 333 exemption request isn't hard to do. There are plenty of approved exemptions already available that you can read. They are publically available in the Federal Register. If you'd like to see my application it is listed as Docket Number FAA-2015-7088. My company's exemption number is 16053. Although I didn't imitate anybody else in writing my exemption request, I wouldn't discourage you from doing so. In fact, I consider plagiarism a sincere form of flattery! I wrote my exemption request using only the guidance the FAA's directions offered. I wanted my exemption to be mine. I planned to use it to write my business plan. I didn't hire a consultant to help me, let alone write my exemption request for me. In this, I would recommend that you follow my lead. Do as much of the exemption request as you can do by yourself. And you can do it, too. I'll offer some pointers later on doing it yourself the way I did it.

When you've written your exemption request, send your petition to the Federal Docket Management System (FDMS) electronically by accessing the public portal: **www.regulations.gov.** After you file your request, be patient. Last I checked, exemptions were taking a minimum of six months. Here's why.

STICK WITH THE PROGRAM AND YOU WILL EVENTUALLY GET YOUR 333 EXEMPTION.

The first step the government takes in processing your exemption request is to post your intentions on the Federal Register for public comment. It took my exemption request two months to be posted. I couldn't control that, and I doubt any contractor can do any better. Your posting may take more or less time than that. After your intention to obtain an exemption is posted, the guidance says that you should hear about your application within 120 days. You'll know your request was posted when you start receiving spam messages from insurance agents and other people offering services to help you conduct your impending business.

Aside from the spam as an indicator that your exemption request has advanced, you can check on your exemption request by writing an email to **333exemptions@faa.gov.** You'll get an answer pretty quickly. I got answers in less than a day. But don't expect to find out much about the status of your particular application in the answer to your request. When I checked on the processing of my exemption I was told it had been received and to "be patient." The FAA was currently examining six thousand exemption requests! In the end it took just over six months from filing for my exemption before I received "the letter" from the FAA. Based on my experience, I'd say six months is a minimum time you can expect it to take to receive an answer to your exemption request.

In my case, the answer I got was positive. The FAA's decision came in the US mail in a manila envelope. Inside the envelope was both my 333 exemption and "Certificate of Authorization" (COA). The exemption listed all I expected, all I asked for and more! A surprise referred me to Docket FAA-2007-3330 at **www.regulations.gov**. I asked for permission to operate four different drones. The docket listed hundreds of drones I can now fly within the scope of my 333 exemption. I still suggest that you include the model(s) of drone you wish to operate under your 333 within your request for exemption. If you get permission to use others, all the better for you.

You probably shouldn't expect to get started flying commercially the day you get your exemption. In my case, it took over a month to insure that my business was in complete compliance with my COA. A requirement to use my COA was to write a General Operating Manual (GOM) for my operation. My GOM includes all the guidance my company personnel need to operate our business within the FAA guidelines. It is a step by step guide. In it as well is a copy of my exemption and COA. Because I wrote my own exemption request, writing my GOM was easy. I drew most of that detail for the GOM from my exemption request. A considerable amount of time writing the GOM was spent lining out procedures, training pilot/observers and insuring that everyone involved in my business was fully read-in on the requirements we would have to meet to comply with our exemption and COA. When it was done I spent some money. I insured and bonded my company. I bought a second drone and spare parts, a computer and software to do the company business. And I made arrangements to conduct all the day-to-day business. I started my marketing, production of our product and procedures for billing the client. I got my employees trained and practiced in doing their jobs. I finished arrangements for payroll and all the other administrative requirements involved in starting a business.

I had my actions planned before I heard from the FAA, but I didn't start spending money making it happen until *after* I got my 333. You should get a head start on these items before you receive your exemption, too. But don't spend money on services you won't need until you have your exemption and your employees (or just you) are trained in GOM procedures and ready to fly.

My 333 request worked out advantageously for me. Your initial contact from the FAA regarding your exemption request could have a less desirable outcome than mine. Instead of an exemption or a COA, you might get a letter describing why you aren't getting either one. This is most likely not a permanent denial of your exemption. The FAA may just need more information from you. You could have forgotten something when you wrote your exemption application. It could also be the result of a delay on the FAA's end. Perhaps a public comment to your posting in the Federal Register requires the FAA to gather some more information from you to answer the public comment. Regardless of why your exemption is delayed or denied, your letter will spell out the issue. It will also give you a deadline to provide that information for them to continue to consider your application. I suggest you meet that deadline to avoid having to start your application all over again.

Avoiding delays generated by inquiries to your posting in the Federal Register will most likely come by carefully crafting your exemption request. This is one of the reasons I took the time to write my own exemption request. I wanted to answer any question that might be asked of me before they were asked. A well thought out exemption request gives the FAA your answers to questions they or the public may have. If your exemption request already answers the question, the FAA will post it in the Federal Register. If you don't answer the questions, don't be surprised if you get your request back for modification.

You'll also get it back if there is something you didn't cover or something about your operation that may be outside of the regulations. When you write your exemption request, it is in your favor to carefully follow the directions. Take your time. Do what the directions say. Read the regulations. Spell out how your operation will follow each part of each regulation. Point out how your operation will make flight operations safer than the regulation calls for. Spell out how exempting you from each regulation will prevent any burden to the American people. You don't have to remember to do all this. Just follow the guidance provided on faa.gov in addressing all the regulations an exemption request requires. The directions list frequently seen errors. Don't make them yourself. The more information about your operation you have on your request, the less likely it is that the FAA will have to come back to you for more information.

Even so, you may see your request denied if the FAA is for some reason dissatisfied with it. You'll have to address that concern when you find out what they don't like. If your exemption request is denied and not just delayed, you're going have to get back in the line to resubmit it. Despite the frustration you may feel though, remember that this process of certifying drone operators is changing day-to-day. Even if you have to start over, remember you are learning from the experience. Care in learning the rules will stand you in good stead when you start flying. Stick with the program and you will eventually get your 333 exemption. That won't happen though if you fly a drone commercially before you have received your exemption and a COA. That's illegal. So follow the rules if you want to get your exemption and fly legally.

HOW DO I WRITE AND SUBMIT A 333 EXEMPTION REQUEST?

At this time, in order to fly a drone commercially you must have in your possession your exemption certificate and COA from the FAA. In order to receive one and begin your drone operations you will have to submit a:

Request for Exemption Under FAA Modernization and Reform Act of 2012, Section 333, *"Special Rules for Certain Unmanned Aircraft Systems."*

Before you get started writing your exemption, go to **http://aes.faa. gov/Petition/look-up-an-exemption.html.** This site will give you an outline of the information the FAA wants to see on your exemption request.

You can read exemption requests that have already been approved at: **https://www.faa.gov/uas/legislative_programs/section_333/333_ authorizations** or as I noted earlier, you can go to **regulations.gov.** Search for *"section 333" faa exemption*. I suggest you go to these sites and read how other drone operators wrote their exemption requests. If you know the name of a specific applicant, like me for example, add that last name to your search. You can see the status of that application and read the exemption request, or comment on it if you like.

PREPARING THE DOCUMENTS

Detailed guidance for writing a 333 exemption is available at:
https://www.faa.gov/uas/legislative_programs/section_333/ how_to_file_a_petition/

In looking through the guidance on the FAA's eRulemaking Portal you will note that you as a commercial drone operator must meet the requirements of 14 CFR § 11.81. You can read this rule and its list of requirements at the FAA's rules website, **ecfr.gov**. In brief, this regulation says that you must include in your 333 petition:

* Your point of contact information.
* The specific sections of 14 CFR from which you want exemption.
* How granting an exemption from each part would benefit the public.
* The extent and reason for relief from the regulation.
* The reasons why granting an exemption from each regulation would not negatively affect safety.

You must also submit a summary that can be published in the Federal Register stating:

* The rules from which you seek exemption.
* The nature of the exemption you seek.
* Any additional views or arguments that support your request.
* The reason you want to operate outside the United States (if such is the case).

Your *333 exemption petition* represents an exemption from the regulations. List those regulations from which you ask relief. These are listed on the first page or two of your exemption request. Prove that you can operate at a level of safety equal to or safer than the regulations require.

The FAA also wants you to describe how the proposed UAS (drone) operation will be safely conducted to minimize risk to the NAS or to persons and property on the ground. You must describe the design and operational characteristics for the type(s) of UAS your company intends to operate. List the make and model of the drones you intend to operate in your request for a 333 exemption. If the FAA decides to allow you more or fewer drones they will let you know in your exemption and COA.

In your 333 application you must also include the operating specifications for the drones you intend to use in your business. There are no FAA approved "Pilot Operating Handbooks" (POH) or "Required Flight Manuals" (RFM) for drones. You can find the specifics about most drones you might buy on the manufacturer's website. If you plan to operate a custom drone it would be a good idea to contact your local FAA Flight Standards District Office (FSDO) for guidance on providing operating specifications on custom drones. Custom drones may even require an FAA airworthiness certificate. Information on acquiring one and determining a new drone's capabilities and limitations is listed in 14 CFR, Part 21 entitled, CERTIFICATION PROCEDURES FOR PRODUCTS AND PARTS.

When you consider your exemption, keep in mind that you cannot use equipment unless it is listed and approved by the FAA in your exemption. When writing your exemption request, include operating procedures and aircraft loading you expect to use. For instance, if you propose to use a photo drone, describe generically what kind of camera(s) you intend to use. If you get too specific, that could be what you'll be limited to using. Rather than use a limiting statement like:

"The company will use the Beeline 'Extra-Special' model 1234a, super digital, gimbal stabilized, ultra-high definition camera."

It might be better to keep from limiting yourself by saying instead:

"The company will use a lightweight digital camera capable of taking video and still images."

If that wording is approved you will have some latitude in the equipment you carry. You will also be able to upgrade your equipment as technology improves or your needs change without having to change your COA. If your drone carries a payload, again list the type and payload generically. If it is designed to carry up to 30 lbs. of fertilizer, will it carry up to 30 lbs. of seed, weed killer and so forth as well? If so, it is better to list a weight and type of content the drone carries and remain less specific about what you plan to have the drone carry.

OPERATING SAFELY IS THE FAA'S MOST IMPORTANT FOCUS.

Throughout your exemption request regularly address how your company will foster safety in all aspects of its operation throughout your 333 application. Describe your operating procedures rather as you would describe the operation of a manned aircraft. Use detail in describing how you will conduct pre-flight inspections, maintenance and repair. If it is available from the manufacturer, include preflight and regular inspection and repair cycles and procedures. Note how you will determine that your UAS is in an airworthy condition before and after the flight. Also address how repair will be conducted, which repair will be done locally and which repair will be referred to the manufacturer.

The FAA encourages the submission of manuals, charts and illustrations to enhance the information provided in your 333 application. Feel free to scan and upload these manuals or separate documents that help describe your equipment and its operation.

Also describe equipment that is supplementary to your drone's operation if it has a bearing on how your business or your drone operates. For example, many drones come with remote controls and viewing devices particular to that model drone. But some of these same drones can use other control boxes and viewing devices. Most can respond to commands from remote control transmitters commonly used with recreational remote controlled model aircraft. Explain how and when devices like these might be used. If it helps the FAA better understand your operation, equipment and systems and how you are going to use them, it has a place in your 333 application.

Your UAS manufacturer's operating specification lists the FCC endorsed transmitter and receiver frequency information. It also contains an FCC approval letter. Either include copies of those in your application or be prepared to follow up you application with a copy of the information if the FAA requests it.

An existing regulation (14 CFR part 91.3 to be specific) already notes that the pilot-in-command is directly responsible for the safe operation of the UAS. Re-iterate this in your 333. List the qualifications required by your company of any pilots who will be directly responsible for the operation of the UAS. The qualifications vary based on how you use your drone. But all commercial drone pilots must have at least an FAA issued pilot certificate, a current flight review and either an FAA medical certificate or they must be healthy enough to possess a state driver's license. Guidance in writing your 333 exemption says that you should define some pilot medical requirements in your exemption request. Medical standards for pilots are outlined in 14 CFR 61.23, but the FAA has not listed the minimum medical requirements specific to a drone pilot. You might consider that pilots flying a manned aircraft with a Sport Pilot Certificate do not require an FAA medical certificate at all. A sport pilot must be in good health and have no medical condition that would disqualify them for a driver's license. That should be all you need to include in your exemption request, and for my company that was the medical requirement my exemption contained.

My exemption requires that the pilot be able to safely fly the proposed flight. It is up to you to determine when your pilot is capable of doing the job safely with your drone. There is currently no minimum number of flight hours or experience required to fly a commercial drone. Setting those requirements is up to you.

I don't have a flight hour based qualification to fly my drones. A single flight hour can represent many flights. My basic trainer runs out of battery power in about seven minutes. My commercial drone has about twenty minutes of battery life. If you intend to set a minimum number of drone flight hours for your pilots to fly your drones, keep that in mind.

When I check out a pilot, I start small. If a current, certificated pilot with a driver's license can fly my little palm-sized drone, I'll trust him or her to show me their stuff with the big drone. Until they can prove to me that they can fly the big drone safely and take pictures they don't fly commercially for Beeline Drones.

Unlike flying a manned aircraft, commercial drone operations under a 333 exemption require both a certificated pilot-in-command (PIC) and a trained visual observer (VO). Regulations require that the pilot/VO team must be in visual line-of-sight (VLOS) with the drone throughout the operation. Note how you will comply with this requirement in your 333 application. My 333 application went into great detail on this item. I created a detailed checklist to describe an entire flying evolution. In it I paid specific attention to the role of the VO. My exemption just noted that a VO should remain within VLOS. Later, my carefully written requirements for the role of the VO I put in my 333 application went into my GOM.

The FAA expects you to describe in your request the intended use of your UAS. Don't ask to do anything contradicting standing regulations. Instead, clearly describe how you will work within current FAA guidance and regulations for UAS to insure that your operation is always in compliance with FAA regulations. Plan to work closely with your FSDO and state that in your exemption request. My COA defined my company's requirement to keep the local FSDO and Automated Flight Service Station (AFSS) advised of all the flying I do. They even want me to report when I don't fly or cancel a flight. "Negative reports are required," says my COA. I also have to notify the Flight Service Station and issue a Notice to Airmen (NOTAM) for every flight and cancel the NOTAM when the flying is either cancelled or completed. You might as well put that plan of compliance in your exemption request. It too, will end up in your GOM.

I believe there is good reason the FAA wants certificated pilots to fly commercial drones. In attaining their pilot certificate, pilots learn the regulations. FAA certificated pilots have also learned and proved they understand the National Airspace System. Pilots know where and when they can and cannot fly. Drone pilots should note that flying drones further restricts operations that would be common and legal in most manned aircraft. Insure that your 333 request addresses those differences. Explain how you will make sure you and your pilots know and comply with the regulations specific to operating drones while complying with all other applicable Federal Aviation Regulations (FARs).

The FAA says a drone's maximum speed is limited to 100 miles per hour. Writing that into your exemption will allow you to fly that fast even if your first drone is slower. The same applies to height above the ground - currently 400 feet AGL. It may be obvious, but state it in your exemption request.

List the minimum weather, flight visibility and distance from clouds where you will fly. If you set lower minimums than "clear and unrestricted visibility," explain why they are safe and what you will do to insure that you never exceed your weather minimums. My exemption limits me to cloud clearance of 2000 feet horizontal and 500 feet below clouds with 3 miles visibility. My advice would be to check other exemptions and see if these are routine. If not, you can ask for lower minimums. Maybe you'll get them.

There is no wind limit specified by the FAA for operating your drone. On the other hand, your drone's specifications probably list a maximum wind speed and gust speed limit. Your experience might cause you to reduce these limits to meet your own capabilities, but your exemption doesn't need to do so. As long as you set your limits at or below the manufacturer's recommended limit, it's likely the FAA will grant your request.

DESCRIBE POTENTIAL HAZARDS YOUR OPERATION MIGHT ENCOUNTER AND HOW YOU WILL MITIGATE THOSE HAZARDS.

This may take some creative writing. You'll have to imagine any operation you could do and any hazard those flights may encounter. Handling emergencies, loss of control of the drone and appearance of a hazard like a flock of birds or a manned aircraft are hazards you should address. This part of your exemption request may be one reason that these 333 request document packages can grow to many pages in length.

Your request should address conducting "risk assessments." I created a risk assessment checklist as part of my exemption request. It too, is included in my GOM and in the back of this book. You might want something similar. Feel free to modify it to meet your needs if you like. A good risk assessment should consider all the hazards to flight at any site before and during a flight. My assessment includes a post-flight checklist as well.

Some drones have "geo-fencing" software. This software interfaces with the drones GPS to keep the drone to flying into airspace prohibited from drone operations. If your drones are so equipped, state that in your exemption request. But also show how with or without "geo-fencing" you still won't violate airspace flying your drone where it doesn't belong.

If after receiving your 333 you seek relief from a regulation – requesting permission to inspect a 500 foot tower when your altitude limit is 400 feet, for example - plan to seek a Civil COA for that operation. The site can be found on FAA.gov or by going to **https://oeaaa.faa.gov/oeaaa/external/uas/portal.jsp**The site notes that the FAA will attempt to process COA requests within 60 days. Your request can be filed electronically from the site.

THE INTENT TO WORK WITH THE FSDO AND AFSS SHOULD BE IN YOUR 333 EXEMPTION REQUEST.

Your 333 petitions' best hope of success and particularly renewal after two years, relies on maintaining a close and collegial working relationship with the FAA through your local FSDO. You should know the FSDO manager and Principal Operating Inspector (POI) for your operation, personally. In fact, I suggest you schedule a meeting with your local FSDO before you plan to conduct drone operations. After that, keep them informed about what you are doing. My COA requires this liaison with the FSDO within 72 hours of any planned flight. Before you conduct any new operation, request guidance for working most effectively with them. My COA noted the regulatory requirement to issue a NOTAM through an AFSS 72 hours, but no less than 24 hours prior to any planned flight operation. This can be done by phone to 1-877-4-US-NTMS (1-877-487-6867).

You should address how you will insure that your operation remains clear of airspace where drones are not permitted to fly. Note how you will deduce the class of airspace in which you will fly and how you will insure that you stay out of airspace where UAS are not allowed. The simplest way to determine the class of airspace in which you plan to fly is to look at a current aeronautical chart. Currently, under a 333 exemption, UAS commercial drone operations within other than Class G (uncontrolled) airspace is prohibited without a COA allowing them. If you wish to conduct drone operation within airspace other than Class G, it will take at least sixty days to find out if the FAA will grant you that permission.

Obviously, operations within a "Prohibited Area" are – as the designation says - prohibited. Logically this includes the PanTex Nuclear Weapons Facility in Texas. Illogically perhaps, it includes George Washington's home at Mount Vernon in Virginia. Know where prohibited airspace exists and belabor the obvious. Express your intention to avoid this type of airspace when writing your 333 request.

All flights, including drone flights are prohibited within 'Temporary Flight Restrictions' (TFRs). Note how you will keep track of the status of

Temporary Flight Restrictions, especially ones that may pop up during your flight. You should also state that you will check with the AFSS immediately prior to any 333 flight. The AFSS will announce TFRs that "pop-up," airspace restrictions or changes and for NOTAMs, that none have appeared that are applicable to your flight. The FAA also has a web application for smart phones called "B4U Fly" which carries current airspace information for drone operators. It graphically depicts "no drone" airspace in real-time in the area of your flight. You should consider acquiring this application and noting your intention to use it in your 333 exemption application. It is also accessible on any computer at **www.faa.gov/uas/b4ufly.**

I HAVE COMPLETED MY 333 EXEMPTION REQUEST. NOW WHAT?

When you have completed your 333 Petition for Exemption, it and any supporting materials should be submitted under a cover letter to the FAA. I read the guidance on the FAA.gov website for writing a 333 exemption request. I created a cover letter for my own exemption request. I've included it for you on the next page for you to see. I got my exemption with that cover letter, but I offer no guarantees that the FAA liked it or that they will accept it as adequate if you use it. But feel free to use it or modify it as you see fit. As a reminder, besides mine there are hundreds of other examples of accepted 333 exemption petitions available to you at:

https://www.faa.gov/uas/legislative_programs/ section_333/333_authorizations

Sample 333 Exemption Cover Letter

date

Docket Operations
M-30, U.S. Department of Transportation (DOT)
1200 New Jersey Avenue, SE., Room W12-140

West Building Ground Floor
Washington, DC 20590-0001

Your Company Business Name – (include corporate structure such as Inc., LLC, LLP, dba, etc.)
Your Business Address
City, State, Zip Code
Attn: List the name and position of the person to whom you wish correspondence from the FAA addressed. You will probably want to list the owner, president, CEO or officer who will be responsible to answering to the FAA regarding company operations.

Subject: Request for Exemption Under FAA Modernization and Reform Act of 2012, Section 333, "*Special Rules for Certain Unmanned Aircraft Systems.*"

To whom it may concern:

"My Company Name, LLC" dba "My Drone Company" requests exemptions from regulations listed in 14 CFR parts:

SUMMARY OF REGULATIONS
Part 21 Airworthiness Certification 21, Subpart H Certification procedures for products and parts,

Airworthiness Certificates Part 61 Certification: Pilots, Light Instructors, and Ground Instructors

Part 91 General Operating and Flight Rules:
    91.103(b)(2) Preflight action
    91.105 Flight crewmembers at stations
    91.109 Flight instruction
    91.119 Minimum safe altitudes

91.121 Altimeter settings
91.151 Fuel requirements for flights in VFR conditions
91.405 Maintenance required
91.407 Operation after maintenance
91.409 Inspections 91.417 Maintenance records

Company name, doing business as "*dba name*," (the company) proposes to operate Unmanned Aircraft Systems (UAS) safely and routinely within the United States National Airspace System (NAS) in the normal conduct of its business. Because of the nature of our aircraft and the conduct of our business, the company requests an exemption for its business operations under FAA Modernization and Reform Act of 2012, Section 333, *Special Rules for Certain Unmanned Aircraft Systems.*

<u>Company name</u> is a <u>*Type of* Corporation</u> focused on providing aviation related services. The company headquarters is located at <u>company address, state, zip code</u>. All contact and correspondence regarding this application should be sent to the attention of the company *Company Officer (CEO, President, etc.)* , <u>Name of company officer</u> at the above address, by telephone at <u>area code and number</u> or by email at <u>email address</u>. (if you have a fax, you might want to put it here, too).

Sincerely,
Name
Title
Company name

HOW DO I SUBMIT MY 333 EXEMPTION REQUEST?
This is right off the FAA.gov website. You may submit your 333 exemption request in the following ways:

(1) Use the Federal eRulemaking Portal: Go to **http://www. regulations.gov** and follow the online instructions for sending your comments electronically. Since your application is submitted to the Federal Register for public comment, your petition will be submitted as a comment.

(2) Mail your petition to:

Docket Operations,
M-30
U.S. Department of Transportation (DOT)
1200 New Jersey Avenue, SE., Room W12-140
West Building Ground Floor
Washington, DC 20590-0001

(3) Use Hand Delivery or Courier to deliver your documents to:

Docket Operations
Room W12-140, West Building Ground Floor
1200 New Jersey Avenue SE
Washington, DC

Hand deliveries should arrive between 9 a.m. and 5 p.m., Monday through Friday, except Federal holidays

(4) Fax your petition to Docket Operations at 202-493-2251.

Your petition will receive a docket number you can use to track your request. If you already have received a docket number before you submit your documents or submit a document later, you must reference that docket number in your request.

WHAT DOES AN EXEMPTION LOOK LIKE?

When the FAA is satisfied with your application it will issue a certificate of exemption and a "Certificate of Authorization" (COA) in the form of a letter. It will be sent to you by US mail. You can see examples of COAs published in the Federal Register. You may be disappointed to find that many 333 exemption requests appear far less complicated than your own. But look at those carefully. You will probably find that the request is for a much simpler operation than the one you are planning. If you are planning a very simple or more restricted operation, using these as an example for your 333 exemption application may make sense.

Take your time and build an application that covers in detail all the operations in which you plan to engage. Writing a less complicated request for exemption, instead of saving you time and effort, could cost you a lot of time and effort later in re-submitting your application and waiting patiently for the FAA to act on your new petition. Writing the request and addressing the regulations for which you are asking exemption will help you both understand and explain in detail how you will run your business. By the time you submit your application for exemption you will have the outline of a good operations manual. And you will also have some good standard operating procedures your employees can use for guidance in doing your business.

An outline for your exemption requests should consist of the list of regulations from which you request exemption. Here's what I did:

* List the designation and name of the regulation.
* Copy the regulation word for word from the eCFR website so the reader can see exactly what the regulation says while reviewing your reasons to be exempted from the regulation.

* State how you will comply with the regulation or state where the regulation is and is not applicable to your operation.
* State how relief from the regulation is good for the American people and not a burden to them or the FAA.
* State how you will provide a higher level of safety in your operation than the regulation currently assures.

WHAT HAPPENS TO MY REQUEST ONCE IT IS SUBMITTED?

When you submit your application the FAA will assign a docket number to your request. You can use it to track progress on your application. There are no deadlines or guarantees for when your docket will be posted. After your request for exemption is posted in the Federal Register, the FAA may contact you for additional information. When I checked on my exemption I found out that it was in line for consideration on a first come, first served basis.

A reminder: you can find a current and updated list of issued exemptions at:

https://www.faa.gov/uas/legislative_programs/section_333/333_authorizations

Refer to this site in preparing your own exemption request.

WHAT CAN I DO IF MY REQUEST FOR EXEMPTION IS DENIED?

A formal document is issued in response to a petition. If your petition is denied, the document should spell out the reason for denial. Although instructions for seeking the exemption should be included, you can go to the following website and get detailed instructions for presenting information or reasons for reconsidering your request. A pdf document outlines the steps for presenting further information and reasons for reconsidering your request. Go to…

http://www.faa.gov/regulations_policies/rulemaking/petition/

Chapter 4

LEARN THE REGULATIONS FOR OPERATING DRONES

The FAA is taking their task of regulating drones in the NAS very seriously. Operating your drone in contradiction to the regulations is considered unsafe and can garner a flight violation. Flight violations can result in stiff fines and penalties, including jail time. You don't have to be a pilot to incur a flight violation. But if you are a pilot, your violation could cause "certificate action" in which you could receive a rather stiff fine and have your pilot certificate suspended or revoked.

Let me make a pitch for why you should follow the rules – besides fines and losing your pilot certificate, that is. The worst thing that can happen by breaking the rules is that you could kill or injure someone, possibly including yourself. Small though drones might be, there is potential for causing injury or death with a drone. A drone going through an airliner's engine for example, could kill a lot of people.

You could also do damage to peoples' property. For this you could be held liable and accountable in civil court. Whether or not you do damage or injury, aviation regulations happen to be *federal* laws. Federal law has teeth in it, and the FAA and NTSB pretty much know how to use those teeth on violators.

More important, over the span of a lifelong career in aviation I have come to respect the rules. I have found through sad experience that they are written in blood. There are no new accidents in aviation, just repeated ones. Rules are written to keep us from repeating mistakes made in the past.

Summary: If you follow the rules, you won't repeat others' mistakes and you'll run a safe operation.

WHAT ARE THE REGULATIONS FOR FLYING DRONES?

Drone operators have a challenge before them so far as regulations are concerned. Whether you are operating under a 333 exemption or under Part 107 there are certain rules and regulations with which you must comply. Official guidance for drone operators are laced throughout the **faa.gov** website as notices, Advisory Circulars, rules, regulations, policies, orders, legal interpretations and guidance. The most stringent of these are the Federal Aviation Regulations. They are laws. You must comply with them. Recommended or "best operating practices" are usually released by the FAA in the form of "Advisory Circulars." They are not law and consequently only advice. You don't have to follow them. On the other hand, failing to follow them has earned more than one aviator a citation for "careless and reckless operation," which happens to be an FAA regulation and consequently, a law.

The first place to look for regulations on the **faa.gov** website is under the tab entitled: *"Regulations & Policies."* Here are listed all the Federal Aviation Regulations or "FARs," confusingly entitled *Title 14, Code of Federal Regulations.* Each aviation regulation is listed as a "part." Critical parts for anyone operating any aircraft –including drones - within the National Airspace System are:

Part 1 entitled, "Definitions and Abbreviations." Its title is self-explanatory.

Part 61 entitled, "Certification: Pilots, Flight Instructors, and Ground Instructors." The pilot of a drone flown commercially must possess an FAA pilot certificate issued under Part 61. Flying under a 333 exemption the pilot must possess a license for a manned aircraft. The pilot must also have a current flight review and a driver's license or FAA medical certificate proving the pilot is healthy.

Drone pilots operating under Part 107 must possess a "Remote Pilot in Command" certificate. It looks like a certificate for a manned aircraft. It must also have a "small Unmanned Aircraft System (sUAS)" endorsement. Part 107 pilots do not require a medical certificate. But the pilot must self-certify that they are physically and mentally healthy.

Part 91 entitled, "General Operating and Flight Rules." This regulation includes rules for operating any aircraft in the NAS. Probably the most important section of Part 91 for a drone pilot is that it addresses the rules and dimensions for various classes of airspace. Drone operators need to thoroughly understand this regulation.

Part 21 entitled, "Certification Procedures for Products and Parts," and its Subpart H, "Airworthiness Certificates, Experimental Certificates." Depending on how they are manufactured and used, drones can fly with or without an FAA Airworthiness Certificate. In operating under a 333 exemption, this part applies to drones because you will have to request an exemption from much of it.

To determine whether or not your drone needs an airworthiness certificate, refer to *https://www.faa.gov/uas/civil_operations/* and specifically to *FAA Order 8130.34.* This order is used by FAA inspectors to issue experimental airworthiness certificates and special flight permits to UAS. If the FAA determines a drone does not present an unreasonable safety risk, the local FAA Manufacturing Inspection District Office can issue a Special Airworthiness Certificate in the Experimental Category with operating limitations applicable to the particular UAS.

Section 333 of Public Law 112-95, Special Rules for Certain Unmanned Aircraft Systems spells out the regulations for which you must seek exemption or relief. These include:

* PART 21 – "Certification and airworthiness requirements for aircraft and parts," Subpart 21.H – "Certificates of airworthiness (except provisional certificates of airworthiness) and special flight permits"
* Part 61 Certification: Pilots, Flight Instructors, and Ground Instructors
* Part 91 General Operating and Flight Rules
  * 91.103(b)(2) Preflight action
  * 91.105 Flight crewmembers at stations
  * 91.109 Flight instruction
  * 91.119 Minimum safe altitudes
  * 91.121 Altimeter settings
  * 91.151 Fuel requirements for flights in VFR conditions

* 91.405 Maintenance required
* 91.407 Operation after maintenance
* 91.409 Inspections
* 91.417 Maintenance records

RULES UNDER A 333 EXEMPTION

Rules for operating under a 333 exemption are determined by how you write you application for exemption and how the FAA deals with it. The FAA decides to allow your request as written, increase or restrict its scope. And, "Yes," the FAA can allow you more latitude in your operation than you ask for. As I said earlier for example, thanks to the COA I received with my 333 exemption I can operate hundreds of drones now, although I only asked for four.

Especially since Part 107 was made law, it is up to you the operator, to spell out specifically how your operation is to be conducted. Although you may receive a blanket exemption with your 333 which may limit you to the same operations permitted by Part 107, do not take this for granted. If you apply for a 333 exemption, spell out in your application exactly how you intend to operate.

When you receive your 333 exemption it will be accompanied by a COA. The COA further spells out the specifics of how you can operate. It may also require extra effort on your part before you can meet the requirements spelled out in it. For example, you may recall that my COA required that I write a General Operating Manual. Your COA may spell out additional requirements like that, too.

RULES UNDER PART 107

Operating a drone in the NAS just got a lot simpler. You don't need a 333 exemption anymore to operate a sUAS. On June 21, 2016 the

FAA released 14 CFR, Part 107 entitled, "Small Unmanned Aircraft Systems." A general breakdown of the regulation was published that week in, "FAA News." You can find it, a synopsis of the regulation or the entire regulation on the faa.gov web site. I include the "FAA News" synopsis. My few comments are separated from the text by [brackets].

* *Unmanned aircraft must weigh less than 55 lbs. (25 kg).*
* *Visual line-of-sight (VLOS) only; the unmanned aircraft must remain within VLOS of the remote pilot in command and the person manipulating the flight controls of the small UAS. Alternatively, the unmanned aircraft must remain within VLOS of the visual observer.*
* *At all times the small unmanned aircraft must remain close enough to the remote pilot in command and the person manipulating the flight controls of the small UAS for those people to be capable of seeing the aircraft with vision unaided by any device other than corrective lenses.*
* *Small unmanned aircraft may not operate over any persons not directly participating in the operation, not under a covered structure, and not inside a covered stationary vehicle.*
* *Daylight-only operations, or civil twilight (30 minutes before official sunrise to 30 minutes after official sunset, local time) with appropriate anti-collision lighting.*
* *Must yield right of way to other aircraft.*
* *May use visual observer (VO) but not required.*
* *First-person view camera cannot satisfy "see-and-avoid" requirement but can be used as long as requirement is satisfied in other ways.*
* *Maximum groundspeed of 100 mph (87 knots).*
* *Maximum altitude of 400 feet above ground level (AGL) or, if higher than 400 feet AGL, remain within 400 feet of a structure.*
* *Minimum weather visibility of 3 miles from control station.*
* *Operations in Class B, C, D and E airspace are allowed with the required ATC permission.*
* *Operations in Class G airspace are allowed without ATC permission.*

* *No person may act as a remote pilot in command or VO [Visual Observer] for more than one unmanned aircraft operation at one time.*
* *No operations from a moving aircraft.*
* *No operations from a moving vehicle unless the operation is over a sparsely populated area.*
* *No careless or reckless operations.*
* *No carriage of hazardous materials.*
* *Requires preflight inspection by the remote pilot in command.*
* *A person may not operate a small unmanned aircraft if he or she knows or has reason to know of any physical or mental condition that would interfere with the safe operation of a small UAS.*
* *Foreign-registered small unmanned aircraft are allowed to operate under part 107 if they satisfy the requirements of part 375. [These are FAR limitations and specifications required of foreign aircraft.]*
* *External load operations are allowed if the object being carried by the unmanned aircraft is securely attached and does not adversely affect the flight characteristics or controllability of the aircraft.*
* *Transportation of property for compensation or hire allowed provided that-*
  * *The aircraft, including its attached systems, payload and cargo weigh less than 55 pounds total*
  * *The flight is conducted within visual line of sight and not from a moving vehicle or aircraft*
  * *The flight occurs wholly within the bounds of a State and does not involve transport between*
    * *(1) Hawaii and another place in Hawaii through airspace outside Hawaii;*
    * *(2) the District of Columbia and another place in the District of Columbia; or*
    * *(3) a territory or possession of the United States and another place in the same territory or possession.*
* *Most of the restrictions discussed above are waivable if the applicant demonstrates that his or her operation can safely be conducted under the terms of a certificate of waiver.*

Remote Pilot in Command Certification and Responsibilities:

* *Establishes a remote pilot in command position.*
* *A person operating a small UAS must either hold a remote pilot airman certificate with a small UAS rating or be under the direct supervision of a person who does hold a remote pilot certificate (remote pilot in command).*
* *To qualify for a remote pilot certificate, a person must demonstrate aeronautical knowledge by either:*
    * *Passing an initial aeronautical knowledge test at an FAA-approved knowledge testing center; or*
    * *Hold a part 61 pilot certificate other than student pilot, complete a flight review within the previous 24 months, and complete a small UAS online training course provided by the FAA.*
    * *Be vetted by the Transportation Security Administration.*
    * *Be at least 16 years old.*
* *Part 61 pilot certificate holders may obtain a temporary remote pilot certificate immediately upon submission of their application for a permanent certificate. Other applicants will obtain a temporary remote pilot certificate upon successful completion of TSA security vetting. The FAA anticipates that it will be able to issue a temporary remote pilot certificate within 10 business days after receiving a completed remote pilot certificate application.*
* *Until international standards are developed, foreign certificated UAS pilots will be required to obtain an FAA issued remote pilot certificate with a small UAS rating.*

A remote pilot in command must:

* *Make available to the FAA, upon request, the small UAS for inspection or testing, and any associated documents/records required to be kept under the rule.*
* *Report to the FAA within 10 days of any operation that results in at least serious injury, loss of consciousness, or property damage of at least $500.*

*   *Conduct a preflight inspection, to include specific aircraft and control station systems checks, to ensure the small UAS is in a condition for safe operation.*
*   *Ensure that the small unmanned aircraft complies with the existing registration requirements specified in § 91.203(a) (2).*

    A remote pilot in command may deviate from the requirements of this rule in response to an in-flight emergency.

Aircraft Requirements

*   *FAA airworthiness certification is not required. However, the remote pilot in command must conduct a preflight check of the small UAS to ensure that it is in a condition for safe operation.*

That's it! You can operate a small drone commercially within Part 107 after you obtain the "remote pilot-in-command certificate with sUAS rating."

You may still plan to submit a 333 exemption request. I think Part 107 has made your job doing so a lot easier. Consider using or altering the preceding requirements of Part 107 to form an outline for your 333 request.

Along with the release of Part 107, the FAA also released Advisory Circular (AC) 107-2 entitled "Small Unmanned Aircraft Systems (sUAS)." As with other references listed for pilot candidates studying for their "Remote Pilot" certificate, Advisory Circular 107-2 should be part of your company's training program. A copy of it is included for reference in the field by our pilots in our General Operating Manual (GOM). It addresses best practices rather than regulatory requirements. These include subjects that all drone pilots should consider in order to reduce accidents, subjects that have long been the grist of manned aircraft safety programs:

* Aeronautical Decision-Making (ADM) and Crew Resource Management (CRM) to make effective use of human resources and crew communication and coordination.
* Use of autopilots and automation in conducting flights.
* Aviation accident prevention through risk assessment.
* Maintenance, inspections, and preflight checks to insure the drone is always in a safe condition to fly.
* Evaluation of the remote pilot's medical condition including their physical and mental capabilities to conduct the flight. This is an important consideration since under Part 107 no formal medical certification is required to operate a drone.

SAFETY OF FLIGHT

The FAA's primary mandate is to insure safe flight operations within the National Airspace System (NAS). Commercial drones are a new and growing technology, but flight safety is old news to the FAA. The 333 exemption, and more recently Part 107 is laid out to help insure flight safety through compliance with the regulations.

Earlier in the book I pointed out that I am having a hard time finding anyone near me operating a commercial drone business. What I should have said is that I am having a hard time finding anyone *legally* operating a commercial drone business. I find that there are plenty of people flying drones illegally. Whether they are doing it out of ignorance or arrogance, they're still operating illegally. If you are one of those people flying drones outside of the regulations, I'd like to ask you to stop. If you are violating the rules, you're not only doing something illegal. You're doing something dangerous. Let me offer an example of how illegal drone operations can be hazardous.

I found the website of a drone operator in my area. The operator was selling photography and videos taken by using his drone, clearly a commercial operation. I have to admit, the videos and pictures on the website were very impressive, very pretty. They were taken at night flying over a major city along a route and at an altitude that I have often flown as an air ambulance helicopter pilot. The shots were made inside very busy Class C airspace not far from a towered airport. In making these videos he was selling, the drone operator caused the drone to pass quite close to two hospital helipads from which I have operated. I think it is unlikely that the operator had a 333 and a COA for these operations. Operating like that endangered safety of everyone he overflew, not to mention the lives of people flying through the airspace in the air ambulance helicopters operating there. Based on the videos and photos I saw for sale, he flew his drone over a crowded city, through occupied, high volume airspace, at night above the four hundred foot drone ceiling. There is no way the FAA would allow him to put so many people at risk and offer an exemption from complying with so many regulations.

I've encountered irresponsible people like this drone operator throughout my aviation career. You can't very often convince them that they are going to kill anyone. You certainly can't convince them that they are going to kill themselves. I found that they couldn't be convinced to do the right thing because it was "right," either. But I could often get their attention and have them do the right thing because they were going to get in big trouble – like go to jail or get a big fine.

Illegal drone operators, please note: the FAA has already levied a $1.9 million fine on a business operating drones in busy airspace – controlled airspace - without FAA air traffic control permission. That operator was only violated for operating his drone in Class B airspace without permission. How much more egregious were the flights of the operator I observed? What kind of penalty would he pay for doing so? I can only guess. So you folks violating the regulations, forget about killing anybody. If you violate regulations, some day somebody will come take all of your money.

Among long experienced aviators and mechanics there is an old saying; "The Federal Aviation Regulations are written in blood." Starting at the dawn of aviation, when people were killed or injured or property got damaged as a result of a flight operation, new rules were written. In all that time, those regulations have come to fill many volumes. In aviation there are no longer new ways to kill yourself, even with drones. Somebody has already done it. And the regulations to stop its recurrence have already been written. So learn the lesson. "Follow the rules. They're usually right." But to follow the rules you need to know what they are. I refer you again to the **faa.gov** and **ecfr.gov** websites. They list all the federal regulations, Advisory Circulars and a host of other publications that will help you in finding the guidelines for keeping your operation safe.

I also recommend that you buy a current copy of the "FAR/AIM" and carry it with you to your job sites. It's a publication available at flight schools, local airports, pilot supply shops and similar places online. The "AIM" part of the publication is the "Aeronautical Information Manual." Like Advisory Circulars, the AIM contains information and operating practices some of which are covered in regulations, but all of which are important for pilots to know.

14 (CFR) is where you'll find the aviation regulations. We'll cover pertinent ones in the next chapter. If you're unfamiliar with them or just rusty, I recommend finding a competent flight instructor or drone operator who knows the regulations. Let them use this book and your FAR/AIM as a guide to teach you the regulations. They'll also help you find the pertinent documents governing your drone operations. Pay for the lessons. They're worth the money.

If you are going to write an application for a 333 exemption you must know all the regulations applicable to your operation. This includes knowing the list of regulations from which you wish to be exempt. In reading your application, the FAA will look for how you will comply with, or operate at a higher level of safety in regard to each of the regulations that apply to your drone operation.

ONCE I HAVE MY 333 AM I READY TO GO TO WORK?

With the 'Remote Pilot" certificate you can always operate under Part 107. But if you want to operate under your spanking, new 333 the answer is *not* an unqualified, "Yes." Your ability to operate under a 333 is limited by what is written in the COA received from the FAA. It describes how and where you can conduct operations in the NAS. You must follow your COA to the letter, so take time to read it carefully. You may find a restriction or something you have yet to do in order to fly under your 333. Incorporate it's directions into your operating manual and procedures. Operations in places other than those described in your COA are prohibited without a new COA that covers the desired operation. Once you submit a request for a new COA, the FAA will evaluate it. By the FAA's own estimate, each new evaluation can take up to sixty days. The FAA has taken a step to speed up airspace authorizations for drone operators. It is called a "blanket" COA. Here's an example:

"FAA Streamlines UAS COAs for Section 333"
Under the new policy, the FAA will grant a Certificate of Waiver or Authorization (COA) for flights at or below 200 feet to any UAS operator with a Section 333 exemption for aircraft that weigh less than 55 pounds, operate during daytime Visual Flight Rules (VFR) conditions, operate within visual line of sight (VLOS) of the pilots, and stay certain distances away from airports or heliports:

* 5 nautical miles (NM) from an airport having an operational control tower; or
* 3 NM from an airport with a published instrument flight procedure, but not an operational tower; or

* 2 NM from an airport without a published instrument flight
procedure or an operational tower; or

* 2 NM from a heliport with a published instrument flight
procedure

The "blanket" 200-foot COA was happily received. But I received an updated "blanket" COA with my 333 exemption that allows operations to 400 feet AGL.

Part 107 represents a blanket release of sorts from many – but not all - of the other restrictions a 333 had built in. Under Part 107 you can actually operate on an airport, instead of miles away from one. You must give way and not interrupt manned flight operations. Besides operating in Class G airspace, you can also operate inside airspace Class B, C, D and E. You don't need a COA to do that as you would with a 333. But you do need permission from the air traffic controlling agencies for that airspace. With anti-collision lights on your drone you can operate in twilight before sunrise and after sunset. Where a 333 requires a visual observer (VO), their use is optional under Part 107. With some limitations Part 107 allows you to carry things on your drone, which would require a new COA under a 333 exemption.

BESIDES THE REGULATIONS, WHERE ELSE SHOULD I GO TO FIND GUIDANCE ON LEGALLY AND SAFELY USING MY DRONE?

A policy with which commercial drone operators should become familiar is **FAA Notice 7210.891, "Unmanned Aircraft Operations in the National Airspace System (NAS)."** It can be found at:

https://www.faa.gov/regulations_policies/orders_notices/index.cfm/go/document.information/documentID/1028629

Policies available there also include:

* Notice 8900.291, Inspection and Maintenance Program Requirements for Airworthiness Certification of Unmanned Aircraft Systems Operating Under 55 Pounds
* Notice 8900.292, Aviation-Related Videos or Other Electronic Media on the Internet
* UAS Temporary Flight Restrictions (TFRs) for Sporting Events (PDF)
* 2007 Federal Register Notice, Unmanned Aircraft operations in the National Airspace System (PDF)
* Notice 8900.313 Education, Compliance, and Enforcement of Unauthorized Unmanned Aircraft Systems Operators
* UAS Certification Status, November 15, 2006, includes FAA focal points for UAS certification project coordination (PDF)
* UAS Certification Status, Optionally Piloted Aircraft and Accidents Involving UAS, August 18, 2008, Revision to AVS Policy (PDF)

NO DRONE ZONES

Drone operations are prohibited in cities and towns within a 30 nautical mile radius of Ronald Reagan Airport in downtown Washington, D.C. The FAA refers to this area as a "No Drone Zone." Drone operations in this area without permission of the FAA are subject to stiff penalties and fines.

DO I HAVE TO REGISTER MY DRONE?

Yes. Whether you use your drone for commercial operations or not, if it weighs more than a half pound (.55 pounds, in fact) it must be registered with the FAA. The FAA says…

> Failure to register an aircraft can result in civil penalties up to $27,500. Criminal penalties for failure to register can include fines of up to $250,000 under 18 U.S.C. 3571 and/or imprisonment up to three years.

Whether you use your drone for commercial purposes or not, you can now register your drone online at **https://registermyuas.faa.gov.** The cost is five dollars. If you use your drones for recreational purposes this one registration and one number will suit for all your drones. If you are using your drones for commercial purposes you will need to register each drone individually. Each drone will have its own number with which it must be marked. When you register online you will be <u>instantly</u> issued a registration number. Affix that number to your drone. Use a permanent marker or place a copy of the number in a battery or other compartment that can be opened without the use of tools.

Before the online registration was available you had to submit a paper registration form of the type used for registering manned aircraft. You may still exercise that route to register your drone. After about six weeks you will be issued an "N" number (so named because it starts with the letter, "N.") You can still obtain an Aircraft Registration Application, AC Form 8050-1 from the FAA Aircraft Registration Branch (AFS-750) in Oklahoma City, or from any FSDO. Unlike the online registration, when you submit the paper form you must also submit evidence of ownership.

After the six weeks or so to process the form you may be issued an "N" registration number as seen on all manned American aircraft. If so, this number must be displayed on your drone or placed in a compartment that can be easily accessed.

When you register your drone, you'll have an opportunity to print the following two pages. I keep copies in the General Operating Manual as a reminder for our pilots. These pages are available on the **faa.gov/ uas** web site.

Remember these simple safety guidelines when flying your unmanned aircraft:

* Don't be careless or reckless with your UAS
* Fly below 400 feet and remain clear of obstacles
* Stay away from other aircraft at all times
* Keep your UAS within your sight
* Don't fly near airports, stadiums, or other people
* Don't fly under the influence of drugs or alcohol
* Keep away from emergency responders

For more information, visit: www.faa.gov/uas/model_aircraft

B4UFLY Smartphone App

* Clear status icon shows flight restrictions and requirements in your current or planned location
* Interactive maps with filtering options
* Available soon in the App Store and Google Play Store

Additional Resources

General Information about UAS:

* www.faa.gov/uas

Information about how to fly safely and responsibly:

* www.faa.gov/uas/model_aircraft
* www.knowbeforeyoufly.org
* www.modelaircraft.org

Information about flight requirements and restrictions:

* www.faa.gov/go/uastfr
* faa.gov/tfr
* www.faa.gov/no_drone_zone/dc

Drone operators must re-register each drone they operate with the FAA Aircraft Registry every three years.

GUIDANCE REGARDING, "UNMANNED AIRCRAFT IN THE NATIONAL AIRSPACE SYSTEM (NAS)"

Commercial drone operators should become familiar with this policy notice, also known as **FAA Notice 7210.891**. This is the guidance that FAA gives its safety inspectors regarding the handling of UAS (drones). The document mostly pertains to large drones capable of flying under IFR. Keep in mind that this guidance was written before the release of Part 107. Consequently the last point only applies to "333" operators.

* UAS pilots shall always give way to manned aircraft.
* Flights must have a ground based observer. "Daisy-chaining" observers or observing from a moving platform must be approved by the FAA on a case-by-case basis.
* The drone must be in ready contact of the pilot and within VLOS of both the pilot and observer.

If you are operating under a 333 and the drone operation you intend to perform does not fit within your current COA, you can expect the FAA to require you to apply for a new, modified COA before you can legally do it.

Further, for 333 operations the PIC must possess an FAA *private pilot certificate* for the following operations:

* Flight in all other classes of airspace.
* Flying under IFR *and* the pilot must have an instrument rating.
* Night operations. (After sunset until sunrise).
* At joint use or public airfields.

* For flights requiring a chase aircraft.
* Any other time the FAA has determined the need, based on the UAS characteristics, mission profile, or other operational parameters.

Chapter 5

LEARN HOW TO FLY A DRONE OR FIND SOMEONE TO FLY IT FOR YOU

HOW CAN I LEARN TO FLY A DRONE?

Regardless of your experience in manned aircraft or lack thereof, it takes time to learn to fly a drone. An increasing number of vendors offer lessons. If you have the money and not much time, this may be the way for you to go.

Another way to learn how to fly your drone is to join the American Academy of Model Aeronautics (AMA). Go to their website **www.modelaircraft.org** and find an AMA airfield and organization near you. There are always people there who can help you learn to fly remote controlled aircraft. Often there are members who have their own drones. Be careful with following this route to learning to fly a drone. You may enjoy yourself so much that you become distracted and start flying all models of remote controlled aircraft.

THE LEAST EXPENSIVE WAY TO LEARN DRONE FLYING IS THE DO-IT-YOURSELF METHOD.

Being a cheapskate the "crawl-walk-run" approach worked for me. If you are already an airplane or helicopter pilot this approach will work for you, too. I started small - with a micro drone. These drones are not much larger than the palm of your hand.

Tiny as they are, they can and probably should be flown indoors. They are hyper-responsive to the controls. It is easy for the pilot to over-control and soon lose control of these little drones. Start slowly with your training with takeoffs and landings. Then ramp up the complexity of the maneuvers. Soon you'll be making takeoffs and landings from a coffee table to a stool and back again. Buy some extra propellers. You'll break some. By the time I broke the four my drone came with though, I had pretty much mastered the basics of flying this little drone. If you want to fly more than seven minutes without recharging a drone, buy two or three. They're cheap.

FLYING A SIMULATOR WILL HELP YOU LEARN TO FLY A DRONE.

That's what I used once I finished breaking the propellers on my micro drone. There are lots of advantages to using a simulator. Among them: you won't break propellers, crash into your furniture or scare your cat. You won't wreck a drone or replace parts while you're learning. You can sit on your sofa flying a simulated drone all day and not have to change or charge a battery.

I purchased a simulator program called "RealFlight 7.5." The program I bought comes with a radio control box with the standard controls you'll use to fly your real drones. The program allows you to learn to fly other model aircraft, if you like. If you intend to fly both rotary wing and fixed wing drones, this program should suit you. If you buy the wireless control box from RealFlight you can actually use it to back up your real drone when you're ready to fly it, too. Not so with the control box with the cable that attaches to your computer. This simulator teaches you how to use the same controller you may end up using on your commercial drone.

With a micro drone and a simulator you'll soon work your way up to a drone large enough to fly outside. You might use the same drone you'll fly commercially for that. But I suggest you buy another trainer that can handle a little wind. Then fly it outside. You can find these trainers online or in a hobby shop for less than $50. For a few extra bucks they'll even have a camera. The camera is just an extra though. Learn how to fly the drone. If you crash it that will not be the bigger deal it would be if you crash your commercial size drone. See what kind of wind you can handle. Buy some spare batteries and propellers with this drone, too. Propeller guards are also available and worth the money as they're cheaper than a new set of props. The more you practice with it, the sooner you'll be ready to move up to your commercial drone. Master the controls flying through increasingly complex maneuvers. Fly around a variety of obstacles, in varying wind conditions. Practice maneuvers you'll probably be doing commercially. For example: if you're going to inspect rooves after a hail storm, practice doing it with your trainer. If you're going to hover up the side of antenna towers, practice doing it with your trainer.

Once you can fly the toy drones and simulator well, it's time to start flying your commercial drone. Take off the expensive camera and mount. There's no need to break them while you're learning. As with the trainers, start slow. Do easy maneuvers and build up to the more complex maneuvers. Fly regularly and build your confidence. Then attach the camera. Learn to use it while the drone is on the ground or on a raised platform like a picnic table. Adding photography to drone flying shouldn't be attempted until you have strong flying skills.

I DON'T WANT TO FLY MY DRONES. I WANT TO RUN MY BUSINESS.

If your business grows as quickly as it has the potential to do, you'll soon find you don't have time to fly your drones. You should be doing the management, anyway – keeping a bevy of pilot/observer teams busy. You need to keep ahead of the marketing, production of a product your customers will want, and all the other jobs associated with a drone business that aren't related to flying. Get ready. You are going to need a growing number of pilots and observers.

Drone pilots are going to be in short supply. So let me make a suggestion for meeting that need. Inexperienced, enthusiastic *manned* aircraft pilots are not at all in short supply. I suggest that you seek them out to fly your drones. You can find them at almost any flight school. A relatively busy flight school will have new and low time private and commercial student pilots in their training pool. Many times those student pilots on their way to an airline job are working low paying jobs scratching up money for their next flight lesson. So here's a suggestion. Go to a flight school. Meet with the chief instructor. Explain your business, your dilemma (a shortage of pilots). If you fly under a 333 exemption you need certificated pilots to fly for you. Let the chief pilot at the flight school – and later your new drone pilots – know that they can make considerably more money flying drones for you than they will elsewhere. Working for you, they'll have the time, money and support to continue flying. Meantime, their training and pilot certificate will come in handy flying commercial drones in the NAS.

There are very few operators with flying positions open who are looking for these inexperienced pilots to fly manned aircraft. But for you, their knowledge of airspace, weather, regulations and the flight service and NOTAM system all make them valuable. And they'll get practice using that knowledge as a pilot in a practical, real-life way. They'll make money doing it. That's a win for both you and your pilots.

Speaking as a drone business owner, I would rather hire an inexperienced pilot who is an experienced and practiced computer gamer, than a pilot like me who has spent a lifetime in the cockpit. I have lots of old habits in flying that don't translate well to flying drones. I also have few of the computer and game remote controller skills that my kids have been developing since they were old enough to hold a game control box.

Drones have been out for a while as toys. My first pilot had experience flying drones already. He had a pilot certificate when he started working with me, too. It was a rare combination but a solid requirement when we had no commercial option to fly drones except to use Part 61 certificated pilots. His brother has lots of drone experience, but no Part 61 pilot certificate. I couldn't use him without a pilot licenses. But now when he gets his "remote pilot" certificate, he can fly for me under Part 107. As a flight instructor I can train him a lot faster and cheaper for that than by putting him in an airplane and teaching him how to fly.

If you are very fortunate like I was, you'll hire a young pilot or two who already has time flying recreational drones. In order to find pilots like that, again I point you toward the American Academy of Model Aeronautics **www.modelaircraft.org**. Lots of members of the AMA have been using remotely controlled flying machines for many years. At their airfields and events you might find some of them who would enjoy working for you as drone pilots. The AMA can also help direct you to valuable links with people involved in model aeronautics, like insurance and bonding agents and builders and designers of custom UAS. Check the AMA website. Find a club near you. Visit and speak with their members. If you find their goals and objectives meet yours, consider becoming a member.

Chapter 6

BUY A DRONE THAT WILL DO THE WORK FOR YOUR BUSINESS

We are presuming here that you have already decided what you want to do for a drone-related business. You already know that a drone can be either fixed-wing or rotary wing. If you didn't do some homework on what drones might fit your needs when you decided to work under Part 107 or when you wrote your 333 exemption request, you need to do that now. You'll be well served by spending time on the internet watching videos to see the capabilities and limitations of each that best suits your needs. Then pick the model that suits your needs – and your budget.

Make a list of models you would consider using. Read and watch reviews about them. Although you may have a long list of drones to pick from, practically you will have to narrow down your choices to one or two. Rather than utilize more of this chapter telling you what category and model drone to buy, let's concentrate on what you should do with the drone you finally choose.

When you choose a model to use I recommend you stick with it. Don't worry about selecting the latest model of drone, or switching away from a perfectly appropriate model for the latest version of the same model. Drone technology changes faster than computer software. You can't even *get* the latest drone technology before the next one comes along. If a new model will save the cost of the drone because its batteries are much cheaper, I would say that is a reason to change. But if you're buying a model because it has a chip in it that recognizes tree branches, and you don't need a drone that recognizes tree branches, I'd say, "Keep your wallet in your pocket." It's better to concentrate on finding a drone or two that will get your job done. The logistical support for that drone or two will be simpler, also. Your costs will be less if you are just buying batteries, spare parts and peripherals like gimbal mounts and cameras for one model of drone.

If you have yet to settle on the drone you want and you can afford the latest drone that has a transponder, radar and sensors to help you avoid birds, then get that drone. But if your budget doesn't allow the fancier model, get the best you can afford that does the job for you. Your drone is an investment worth protecting.

Part 107 doesn't require what 333 calls a "VO," (Visual Observer). But you should consider how you will use an observer because there are just some jobs that need one or two observers. Consider the guidance of the 333 regulations. The pilot and observer must maintain verbal communications while flying the drone. The FAA does not consider that a cell phone is an appropriate means of staying in contact. That suggests that radios are the way to go. A pilot can't operate a push-to-talk (PTT) radio while their hands are on a control box, so the pilot should have a radio and headset. The observer on the other hand, could probably do fine with a PTT radio. The team should also be equipped with a hand-held radio that will allow them to monitor aviation frequencies. You can buy them at the pilot supply shop where you get your FAR/AIM.

AS A DRONE OPERATOR YOU ARE EXPECTED TO MAINTAIN SITUATIONAL AWARENESS.

You'll need that radio. Although with a 333 you are restricted from operating a drone near airports or their instrument approaches, even flying under Part 107 avoiding air traffic is your responsibility. Even if you're not flying near an airport, crop dusters and helicopters often fly low enough where drones can be a hazard. Know and monitor the local airport Common Traffic Advisory Frequency (CTAF), tower frequency, air traffic control (ATC) frequency or en route frequency that aircraft may use in your area. Be prepared to use those frequencies to warn air traffic of your operation and if your drone gets out of your control.

The FAA expects you to keep a record of all your flights. Experienced pilots are well familiar with logging their flight time. Logging drone flying time is not much different than logging any other VFR flying. It just doesn't count toward training and currency for manned aircraft. A pilot's logbook can be used to record the date, drone model, registration number and time flown along with a comment about the flight you did. You as a business owner should keep the information about the flights flown in connection with your business, too. While you're at it, buy a logbook to keep track of the hours your drone flies, as well as the maintenance and modifications you do to your drone.

Chapter 7

SET UP THE BUSINESS

HOW DO I KNOW MY BUSINESS WILL BE VIABLE?

Once you have determined the business you want to do, you have to make sure there is a market for that business. You can have the best company in the world but it won't work if you don't have customers. Do a market survey before you start or even settle on a business you want to start. A market survey's purpose is to confirm that your business will have customers. Once you find out where there's a need for your service, build a business to service it.

There are many ways to do a market survey, but let me tell you how I did mine. I put up a website. A website has other utilities to it, but one of its functions is as a marketing tool. I figured that if I put up a site advertising the product I wanted to sell, I'd get a response to it whether I was ready to sell that product or not. I was not, so I was a little concerned that potential customers would be disenchanted with me for offering a product I couldn't provide. That didn't happen. It turned out that nobody else was even offering my product. The people who responded to my website were happy to hear that I intended to offer my service and product soon. They were willing to wait. More important, there were *lots* of customers waiting! So I set up my business.

I'm not very savvy technologically. I didn't think I could do my own website. Having done one now however, I can tell others like me that setting up a website is no big deal. It started with obtaining a web domain. That also is easy and inexpensive. The domain I used had a website creation tool as part of the service. There are probably better webpage design tools, but theirs worked fine for me. It didn't take long for me to build my own website. Two days after I had my domain, **http://beelinedrones.com**, I had a website designed and "live" on the web. Visit it and let me know what you think. I designed a page for inquires and quotes. Within twelve hours of the site going live I had enough business to keep a half dozen drone teams busy. And I didn't even have my 333 exemption yet to get them busy. That told me I was in the right place to see success in my new drone business.

ANYTHING YOU CAN DO TO GET YOUR COMPANY NAME BEFORE CUSTOMERS IS A GOOD IDEA.

One way to grow sales I have always relied upon is the old fashioned, "cold call." Lots of people are afraid to do that. A "cold call" is when you approach a potential customer without an invitation and present them with the opportunity to do business with you. We are all afraid of rejection. We don't want to hear the word, "no." But oh how sweet it is when we hear a "yes," especially an enthusiastic one. If you are enthusiastic about what you have to sell, don't be surprised when someone is enthusiastic about buying it.

That's another problem with cold calling. I find that most people who "cold call" are not prepared to handle a "yes." You need to train yourself to expect a "yes." If you're selling a drone service, let the customer know what they're buying. When someone is prepared to buy, *stop selling*! You got your, "yes." Close the deal right there. Have a drone with you to show to the customer. Be prepared to do the ground work on the spot. You can't fly, but you can get a contract signed, a payment made and do your site survey. If there is ground work that can be done like still photographs or hand-held video, be prepared to do it right then. With my business we detach the camera and do some of our camera work from a handheld device before we even have to fly. Invite them along as you photograph what you're doing by hand. Find out what the customer wants. Take the pictures they want to see. Then provide them in a timely manner to examine.

If they want to watch you work, do a weather and airspace check while they watch. If you're working under your 333, you can even file your NOTAM for the flight if it looks like the next day's weather and other circumstances will accommodate a flight. I have electronic flight charts and maps on an iPad. I also have the FAA's web application "B4U Fly" on my iPhone. I show the customer the airspace that comes into play with the flying we'll be doing for them. Even if they don't understand everything they're seeing, they realize that they are doing marketing in an entirely new and innovative way.

The key to closing a deal is to have a plan ready to execute and provide the service as soon as the customer says, 'yes.' There's no time for buyer's remorse. That is also a good time to take payment. I take credit cards and process them right on my phone. If things work out just right, by the time I send an invoice to the customer it is already marked "paid."

DON'T BE AFRAID OF A "COLD CALL"

Get face-to-face with your clients. People like to see the folks with whom they are dealing. Looking someone in the eye, shaking their hand and expressing yourself with body language all trumps a phone call. It's also harder to turn down someone who is looking right at you than it is to hang up a phone on a salesman. And it's easier for your customer to re-member you when they've actually met you. If you can't close a deal on the first meeting, you may meet that person in the grocery store some-time later and close a deal there. That's not something that will happen if all they know about you if from a phone call.

Target your customer base. If you're doing what I do working with real estate related business, go talk to realtors. If you're working in the oil fields, talk to the base manager of the company you want to do busi-ness with. Before you show up at your customer's office, post a sample of your product on your website. When you meet your target customer, carry your tablet computer. Call up your website and show them the video you loaded. A video is the best way to show your customer what you can do for them. Leave a business card and point out your web address so they can take another look at what you have to offer. They might even show it to their partners. Send a follow up email with the link to the site you showed them. And follow up with them person-ally. Once you meet someone who might want your business, visit with them again. Call them from time to time. Remind them that you still want their business. One of the strongest tools for closing a deal is persistence.

Utilize your corporate entity you defined before you filed for your 333 exemption. Your state's secretary of state, your bank and the IRS are most interested in seeing how you have structured your company. All three are immediately interested in your cash flow. Cash flow deter-mines success or failure of your company. Your bank and a good CPA should be on your side of the cash flow equation. They'll help you set up your system for setting aside and paying your taxes on time, too.

Legitimize your company. Nothing validates your business like pleasing your customers. Pleasing your customers with a good product and good service will spread the word that you are the company to work with. Anticipate what your customer will need and have a plan for providing it to them. Show them how you plan to provide the services they need. Show them the value of your product. Show them the cost of your service. Give them an estimate and stick with the contracted price.

Your customers may not know your business well enough to tell you what they need until you show them what you can do. Provide the customer with your plan to service them. Let your customer know that they are important.

REMAIN OPEN TO NEW AND DIFFERENT WAYS TO UTILIZE YOUR DRONES.

Listening to the customer's ideas may lead to new customers and even a new line of business. Tell them and then show them that you can do what they need and want. And as I mentioned earlier, concentrate on giving more than you expect to get. Whether from this customer or another you'll certainly get more than you gave. When you do a good job, don't be shy about asking customers to tell their friends. Ask them for an endorsement that you can use in your advertising and to show potential customers. Likewise, when you make a mistake or don't meet the mark, apologize and do what you can to mend fences. Never leave a customer unhappy or dissatisfied if you can help it. As the saying goes, "If a customer is happy, they'll tell their friends. If a customer is unhappy, they'll tell everybody."

Make yourself unique. In the drone business, that's probably easier to do now than it will be later. Right now almost any commercial drone operator can start off an advertisement by bragging that, "We are the only drone based business that…" Then fill in the blank. You may not be the only drone based business in the country that does what you do, but you are possibly the only one in your state, region or city who does what you do. Capitalize on that. Establish your reputation as THE company to go to before there are others competing for the title.

Let your customers know what makes your company unique. If there is competition, show customers what sets you apart from other businesses – without 'plugging' your competition. Right now you can focus on what sets drones apart from manned aircraft or other vendors that do your business in some fashion. One of those differences is price. You might consider showing them what your service would cost with a manned aircraft to illustrate how unique drones are. And drone related businesses are still unique. Capitalize on it with customers.

SHOW YOUR CUSTOMER THAT YOUR OPERATION IS SAFE, LEGAL AND PROFESSIONAL.

And if the customer mentions it, acknowledge that drones have gotten some bad press. Near misses with aircraft and privacy issues have made the news. If your customer has concerns, explain why those issues are not an issue with you and your company.

Let customers know that your company is professionally operating under an FAA exemption, if you have one. If you're operating under Part 107, let the customer know you're "operating within FAA regulations and guidelines." I show our 333 exemption number on our logo and company card, forms and documents. Point it out to your customer and tell them what it means. Note that your company employs FAA certificated pilots. Even if it's the "remote pilot" certificate, every commercial drone operator has to use certificated pilots. But every drone company should let their customers know that. Proudly list the level of training and experience your pilots' certifications represent, too. Bragging is totally approved when you're talking about your business.

DESIGN AND REGISTER A LOGO.

Beeline Drones ™

As soon as you register your corporate entity you will receive unsolicited emails from companies who want to provide another service for you that you can do for yourself. Registering a logo is one of those services. A logo sets your company apart and gives it recognition just by people seeing the logo. Look at any logo for a successful company. The Apple Computers "apple" logo for example says who they are without a word. The Coca-Cola logo's one word, "Coke," trademark now speaks for the company all over the world. The Nike "swoosh" trademark has come to mean what the company stands for, whether the logo is on a cap, a tennis racket, t-shirt or a tennis shoe.

You can create a Trade Mark for free just by putting "TM" after your logo. It alone offers you certain rights and protections you might expect from a registered trademark or logo. Like a copyright, a registered trademark is filed with the federal government. Registering your logo can be easily and inexpensively done without any help from a consultant. Go to the website for the US Patent and Trademark Office (**www.uspto.gov**). It is easy to accomplish registering a trademark or logo by just following the steps on the website. Once it is registered, your trademark can be followed by the distinctive ®. You can't use the symbol unless you have indeed registered your trademark with the US Patent and Trademark Office.

My company logo is a picture of my baby granddaughter in a bee Halloween costume. It is unique, which is one thing your logo must be. It should speak for your company. That little girl is the "bee" in Beeline Drones. I've been told by critics that the picture makes my company seem downhome and unsophisticated. I thank the critics, not mentioning that is exactly what I was aiming for. "Wendy's Hamburgers" bears the name and is represented by a stylize picture of the founder's daughter. The inference about my logo being too "down home" infers that I should choose a logo that makes my company look more polished. From my perspective, "down home" works better among my rural neighbors in Central Texas, than "polished" does. A logo speaks for your company. Choose one that portrays you and your personality as well as what you do. When you get a logo or trademark, put it on your equipment, the door of your company cars and trucks, your employees' uniforms and caps, coffee cups for your customers and all your advertising including your website and business cards. "A picture is worth a thousand words," you might have to use to remind people who you are.

Reduce your company's risk. Drones are virtually brand new to most of your customers. They may be shy about using them based on some perceived hazard or something that made them think using drones is risky. Let your customers know at the outset that your operation is "bonded and insured." In fact, some customers require both a bond and insurance. With the growth of commercial drone businesses the insurance industry has stepped up to provide these services. Reputable companies are vying to bond and insure your company. They're no harder to find than by making a computer search using the words, "drone insurance." Shop the growing network of insurance companies and you'll save yourself some money. Buy the insurance you need. If you customer wants more insurance or a bond, make the up-charge part of your price quote.

Make Money With Drones. The value of a safe and professional operation, the good work of your employees and your customers' good will is all noted. But if your company doesn't make a profit, you're out of business. Simply put, the way to insure that your company will make a profit is to charge more than the service costs you. In setting rates for your service, don't just charge more than you spend to provide your service.

CONSIDER THE "PERCEIVED VALUE" OF WHAT YOUR COMPANY OFFERS.

Here is an example of perceived value. You might say that a haircut is just a haircut. But at a hair salon on Rodeo Drive in Beverley Hills, California a customer will pay $1300 for the same haircut a customer can get in a barber shop in my little Texas town for $13. I propose to you that the $1287 difference in the cost of those haircuts is strictly "perceived value." The customer who pays $1300 for a haircut sees enough value in getting their haircut on Rodeo Drive to pay so much more than getting their hair cut elsewhere.

The lesson here is that when you set your rates, don't short change yourself. Charge what your customer can see as perceived value in using you and your service. If you are the only company that offers this service, the customer sees perceived value in the uniqueness of working with you. Emphasize that his friends and competition will see a product showcasing his business in a way they have never seen before.

You are unique, and by their association with you -- so too are your customers. Because you produce a product that makes your customer look better than their competitors, there again is an opportunity to charge for perceived value.

If using your company doubles the customer's profits, now you have a measure of exactly how much all that perceived value is actually worth. Success will convince your customer that your product is worth the cost. So do all you can to help them be successful. You know how to use a drone. They don't. Use it to advantage that expresses the perceived value you offer. That isn't really as difficult to do as you think. People see less value in things that cost less than they're worth. Likewise, people are willing to pay more for the same item they can get at a lower price because they perceive that a more expensive item is somehow "better" than a less expensive similar item. And that may be true in some cases. But how much better can one watch, or a pair of tennis shoes or a car be that allows one vendor to charge many times more than another?

Here are two adages from professional sales people that apply to perceived value. "You aren't selling the steak, you are selling the sizzle." Find out what it is about your business that makes it sizzle – that makes it attractive. Then sell that. And the other adage from professional sales that comes to mind is, "If you want to make more sales, raise the price." People will pay more for things in which they perceive higher value.

The manager is accountable for the success or failure of the company. As the owner and manager, _you are ultimately responsible for everything your business and its employees do or fail to do._

Your primary job is to run the business so that it makes a profit. Your job every day is to pay attention to the mechanics of running your business.

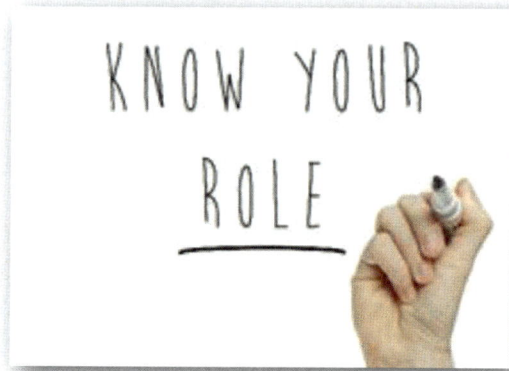

Regardless of who does the flying, the camera work, the video editing, the web-based product delivery, the accounting or administrative tasks, you – the manager - are ultimately responsible for producing a product that meets the customers' needs and makes a profit in doing so.

The bugaboo in the management schools is "micro-management." In brief, "micromanagement" is when a manager breathes down the neck of their employees challenging everything they do. It shows the employee that the manager doesn't trust them to do a good job. Better management recognizes that people work best when they are happy, trusted, empowered and enthusiastic. I encourage that. I appreciate it myself when the management trusts me and backs my decisions. Treat your employees just as you would want to be treated by your boss. At the same time, there has to be a point between micro-management and no management where a manager remains actively involved in the company and how it does business. In managing your company you have to be involved and cognizant of what is happening in your business every day, regardless of your management style. That authority cannot be delegated.

Managers often fail because they do not let their employees know what is expected of them in a clear and understandable way. I suggest that you and your employees set up a Standard Operating Procedure (SOP) for everything your company does. Include your employees in the construction of these SOPs. In them the people who do the work explain how they do it. An SOP should be able to explain to a new employee how to do a given task. SOPs should be incorporated into a GOM. You may have managed businesses that do not work this way. But the FAA expects commercial aviation operations to operate under a GOM. Although currently there is no requirement for drone-related businesses to do that, the FAA *prefers* that even your request for the 333 exemption be submitted as a GOM. A GOM is invaluable as your company grows. New employees who don't know how your company runs, and old employees who forgot (or never knew) how your company runs will have specific directions if your company uses a GOM.

As the manager, you should hold your employees accountable for knowing your company GOM, and operating in ways it standardizes within your company. Every employee of the company should be able to refer to their own copy to see the company approved way to do any task. Because your procedures for doing any given job will change, be sure your GOM is updated regularly. I serialize my GOM with the valid date of the document on the front page. When I change the GOM I send an electronic copy to everybody in the company, highlighting in bold the changes made since the last GOM. Then I check to see my employees have and are using the latest GOM. In manned flight operations I have seen the FAA do the same kind of audit. A pilot with an expired GOM was cited and the company fined. I haven't seen that happen in my drone operation yet, but my company and I are prepared in case it happens.

QUALITY ASSURANCE IS THE LAST STEP IN THE PRODUCTION PROCESS BEFORE YOUR CUSTOMER SEES YOUR PRODUCT.

It is up to you to see that the product your company produces is just what you, the owner/manager wants that customers to see. If this responsibility is delegated, make sure you keep a close eye on what the delegated quality assurance representative of your company is sending to the customers.

WATCH THE MONEY!

Here's some valuable advice from a lifetime in business and from better business people than me. "Whoever controls the purse strings, controls the company." It's your company. It is your responsibility to control income and expenses. Regardless of who does the credits and debits and enters the payments, invoices and liabilities into the accounting sheets, take the time to watch the books yourself every day. Examine the profit and loss statements (P & L) whenever they are produced. Accounting programs have made this P & L step easily enough produced to create one daily, weekly, monthly or whenever you wish.

Examine payments and bills. Watch the bank transactions carefully. Know where and how your money is being spent. Keep track of invoices, payments to the company and insure the entire payments reach your company bank account. A company I own or manage has to be pretty big and busy before I'm not the guy signing the checks. Know what each check represents. And don't let liabilities like unpaid invoices stay on your books for long, either. Pay your bills on time. Unpaid bills of yours are as big a liability to you and your company as unpaid invoices by your customers. Both represent money you do not have.

Write and update your budget. Most businesses go out of business within the first year. Most of them go out of business because they are undercapitalized. As important to the success of your business as a business plan, is a budget. You need to know what you are trying to accomplish. That's the business plan. But you need to plan for how much reaching those goals will cost. That's a budget. You also need to set goals for what amount of profit you expect to make. Plan so you will know how much money you will need to make, then plan for how much money you expect to make. Your budget will show you the difference between the two. That difference is called, "profit," or "loss."

Lay out a matrix for where the money will go when you make it. Know how much it will cost to start your business. Know how much it will cost to conduct daily operations. List everything that will require your resources to start and continue operations. Build a cushion into your operation to insure you always have the funds you need to keep operating, even when income disappears for a time.

One thing that is drawing people to start a drone-related business is that it does not cost a great deal of money to get started. Even so, start up your company and stay within your budget. If during startup you spend more than you make you need to know how long you can do that based on the capital you saved to start your business. If you don't make money though, regardless of how you capitalized your business you won't be in business for long. You can always alter your budget based on your income. You can save yourself a lot of money if you do most of the legwork yourself. We've already noted some of the things you can do for yourself that could save you many thousands of dollars on startup costs, starting your business yourself: write your own 333 exemption request; incorporate your own company; create and apply for a logo yourself using the guidance on the government website; shop for and buy your own drone(s) that meet your budget as well as your operational requirements; know your equipment, how it works and what spares you'll need; shop for all your logistical support items - spare parts, batteries, office equipment and supplies. Everything.

IN REVIEW
This is how you start a business in the dynamic and burgeoning drone industry:

1. Figure out what you want to do as a business.
2. Obtain a corporate entity.
3. File for and obtain an FAA exemption.
4. Learn the regulations.

5. Learn how to fly a drone, or find someone to fly it for you.
6. Buy a drone that will do the work for your business.
7. Set up the business.

Post those steps somewhere you can see them every day until you have your business up and running. As your business takes off, take the time to perfect the processes in how you do your business. When the processes you set up in your business work, duplicate them.

This last piece of advice has been invaluable in my life, so I pass it along to you here. Take the time necessary to thoughtfully and sincerely set your own near and long term goals. Write down what you want to accomplish and where you (and your business) will be one, two, five and ten years from now. Write a date by which you plan to accomplish each goal. A goal without a date is called a dream. I carry my goals on a business card in my wallet. As with any plan, I update this little card as I accomplish these goals. You will find yourself updating it more often than you might think right now. You will see what happens as I did since I put my goals into my wallet for the first time decades ago. I was surprised to find that I achieved all of those objectives I wrote down, and I accomplished them in half the time I originally expected to accomplish them.

Opportunities like those opening up with drones come around once in a lifetime. I encourage you here again to seize this opportunity! This is your chance to take advantage of perhaps the most dynamic prospect to happen in your lifetime. Keep this book handy. Highlight it. Use it as a guide. Share it with people you want to see succeed. And contact me if I can help you. Join me in this rising wave of business. Now is the time to get busy!

Patrick Shaub
President
Beeline Drones
Marble Falls, Texas
2016

OPERATIONAL ANNEX TO:
"Making Money With Drones."

By

Patrick Shaub

BEELINE DRONES
Job Site Risk Assessment

Date: _____

Pilot/Observer: _____

Flight Time logged on this job: _____

_____

<u>Job Location:</u> *(address, latitude/longitude and/or description).*

The purpose of the Risk Management Assessment is to document your evaluation of the job site and record the information you need to plan a safe and effective flight. The information you record will help us to plan safe flights and train others based on the flight you conduct.

Use your "site assessment" and this "risk management assessment" to create a "mitigation plan" to be submitted to the company for each job you do. Note the hazards and write down your plan to mitigate them. If a risk cannot be effectively and safely mitigated, *DO NOT CONDUCT THE FLIGHT!*

BEELINE DRONES
Site Assessment

If operating under our 333, a Notice to Airmen (NOTAM) must be filed no sooner than 72 hours and no later than 24 hours before the flight is made.

You may not fly a drone:

* From a moving vehicle or vessel.
* Near military or federal facilities, certain stadiums (see NOTAMs/TFRs), emergency services vehicles or stations, power plants, dams, electric substations or industrial complexes.
* In a Temporary Flight Restricted area (TFR) or Prohibited Area or near the Disney resorts or inside the Washington DC restricted zones and other Special Use airspace.
* Near wind farms, oil refineries or along pipelines without permission.
* Between sunset and sunrise (i.e., no night operations).
* Under 333: Within 5 miles of a towered airport, Within 3 miles of an airport with an instrument approach or 2 miles of a heliport or 2 miles of a heliport.
* Under Part 107: remain clear of aviation and other drone operations without company approval.

PRIOR TO CONDUCTING ANY FLIGHT,

The pilot and observer shall walk the site or otherwise evaluate the job site. If this is impossible or ability to walk part of the site is limited, the pilot and observer shall walk to all points around the site from which they shall observe and control the drone. During the site survey the following factors will be considered.

** Be sure to note other factors not listed that may affect or detract from the safe and efficient completion of the job.

FACTORS TO NOTE AT THE JOB SITE:

Beeline's company weather minimums are 3 miles visibility and 500' below and 2000' horizontally from any clouds

* Check MSL Altitude of the site.
* Operate within density Altitude & ambient temperature limitations.
* Check weather from a company approved source like the National Weather Service or Flight Service.
* Note the following at the site: Cloud types & height, horizontal visibility, wind direction, velocity and gusts, presence of rain, thunderstorms, fog, smoke or any phenomena that will limit visual observation or aircraft control.
* Note the presence of Air traffic. Set the VHF radio to the appropriate air traffic frequency for the job site area.
* Insure clearance from people, animals or livestock in the open.
* Avoid Bird Hazards (especially raptors, birds in flocks and migratory birds like geese, ducks, doves, pigeons etc.).
* **Protect other peoples' privacy & be respectful of people at the job site**:
* Insure people in the area of the job are notified about your presence.

* Do not overfly or photograph occupied areas, especially pool or areas enclosed by a privacy fence.
* Avoid structures or property that could be damaged if struck by our drone.
* Avoid noise sensitive areas.
* Other sensitive areas like occupied churches, cemeteries, historical sites, wildlife refuges, hospitals, etc.
* Drone prohibited areas like federal or military facilities, power plants, electric substations, dams, national parks, emergency services facilities or scenes (Fire, Police and EMS) and oil, chemical and other industrial complexes.
* Note hazards to flight like wires, antennas, towers and other obstructions to the drone's takeoff, landing, "home" function course and landing path.
* Roads: Note type and frequency of vehicular traffic .Avoid vehicles both static and moving.
* Note and avoid construction or farm equipment.
* **Cease operations in the vicinity of crop dusters, low flying airplanes/helicopters, and other drones.**
* Note condition of the terrain (swampy, dusty, rocky, and agricultural) and the traffic-ability for vehicle and foot traffic to recover a downed drone.
* Note and plan emergency landing sites if flying near lakes, ponds, streams and other bodies of water.
* Take note of height and types of vegetation should an emergency landing be required.
* Walk and examine the flight path and its traffic-ability.
* If you cannot walk the flight path, plan safety areas, observation points and control points along the intended flight path.
* Plan and examine Emergency Landing sites you will use in the event one is required anywhere on the route.

Starting the day before the flight, answer the following questions and re-check the day of the flight:

A NOTAM can be filed by calling: (1-877-4-US-NTMS) or (1-877-487-6867).

A NOTAM is required for 333 operations.

Otherwise, a NOTAM can be filed if the pilot assesses filing one will increase the safety of the operation.

The NOTAM must be closed out after the flight or in the event the flight is cancelled.

If one is required, has a NOTAM been filed no later than 24 to 72 hours before this flight? If not flying under the rules of our 333, cancel the flight until the requirement is met.

Have you checked the airspace?

> KnowB4Ufly
> VFR and IFR sectionals
> Airports, Heliports, Glider ports
> Appropriate instrument approach plates
> Airspace other than Class G
> IR/VR routes
> Special Use Airspace
> Drone prohibited areas

AFSS (Flight Service @ 800-WX-BRIEF / 992-7433):
Did you call Flight Service or consult a National Weather Service site to check:

Weather, winds, ceiling, visibility

Weather forecast for the flight.

Are these observations above company and personal minimums?

NOTAMs for our NOTAM and operations that would inhibit or raise the risk of our safe operation.

Status of Military Training Routes (VR and IR routes).

Status of TFRs

Obstructions posted o charts.

List the appropriate air traffic frequencies for the area you're working:

Have you operationally checked your handheld aviation transceiver?

Have you done a communications/radio check as a team?

Has permission of the land/property owners around the site been obtained in writing?

Is the area of your flight marked with cones, tape or otherwise restricted from interference?

Are curious people or gatherings of people present? If so, how have you mitigated the risks they pose?

** Is the flight within a Special Flight Rules Area - Washington, D.C., The Hudson River in New York, Luke Air Force Base and other areas around the United States? Flying within these requires special procedures. Check FAA.gov for updates on these areas.

Will the pilot and observer have unobstructed line-of-sight of the drone throughout the planned flight?

Will the pilot and observer have clear, unobstructed verbal communication with each other at all points of the flight?

Can the pilot avoid other aircraft and can the observer(s) restrict or warn persons, vessels or vehicles that may enter the flight path?

A preflight inspection of the drone and its control box and their interface is required before each flight.

Is the pilot satisfied that the drone is in 100% safe and serviceable condition? If "no," do not fly until repair and a functional test flight is successfully flown.

Can you describe how you will maintain altitude below a maximum of 400 feet above the ground?

Can you complete all operations during daylight hours?
(*Per company policy, "Flights must not begin before sunrise nor continue after sunset"*).

Are there any other drones working in your area?
(*No more than one drone will normally be permitted at any one time within the same block of designated airspace without management permission*).

Did you turn off all personal electronic devices?

NOTE: Except for devices used to call between the pilot and observer, cell phones, radios, devices which use earbuds, head phones or other similar distracting devices should be turned off or disconnected before flight operations begin.

Are there high voltage electric lines, radar dishes or other high power electrical facilities in the area which may interfere with the radio control devices transmitting between the drone and the pilot?

*   Other factors I saw during my site assessment are listed here.

RISK ASSESSMENT MAP

*   Use this space to map the area and hazards you noted during your assessment.

POST FLIGHT CHECKLIST:

Review Assessment Checklist and note changes that developed during the flight ("Flight was cancelled when winds increased mid-way through the flight," for example)

Record flight time on the risk management assessment sheet and in the drone's logbook.

In keeping with 14 CFR, section 61.51 the pilot shall maintain a record of each flight (in a personal logbook or other acceptable record).

Do a post-flight inspection on the remote controls and aircraft for wear or damage. Initiate required repairs.

Complete this Safety Mitigation Plan and turn all paperwork associated with the flight into company management.

RECHARGE YOUR BATTERIES

YOU GOT YOUR EXEMPTION!

Do simulated flights until you are assured the product can be produced by the company and delivered to meet company standards.

Check out pilot and observer teams for competence in flying the job, knowledge of the GOM, ability to handle communication and pre and post flight procedures.

Copy pilot's medical if required by company's 333, and pilot certificate for company files.

Check pilot's logbook includes all company training. Copy their contents to company files.

Log all company flights for audits.

Insure & bond the company, its aircraft, vehicles and operations.

Make a liaison visit to the local FSDO regarding: Introduction to FSDO personnel Requirements for regular operations:

* Review the company GOM Requirements to keep the FSDO informed about our operations
* Discuss conduct of operations near airports/heliports.
* Acquire and prepare logistical support.

Ensure the company has a Drone kit plus a spare including:

Spare props, batteries, chargers

Inter-team radios & headsets

VHF transceiver for aircraft communications

Company forms, "Drone Operations" warning signs, traffic cones, "caution" yellow tape.

Checklists runoff and ready for coming jobs

Review *current* GOM, 333 Exemption and COA with pilot/observer teams.

Issue assignments to pilot/VO teams.

INDEX OF DEFINITIONS

333 – References Public Law 333 from which exemptions to this public law create the "333 exemption" from FARs and allow commercial drone operations.

AC – Advisory Circular

ADM – Aeronautical Decision Making

AFSS – Automated Flight Service Station provides preflight, planning, inflight and post flight services to pilots such as filing, opening and closing of flight plans, preflight and inflight weather briefings and providing airspace and in-flight alerts and airspace information to pilots.

AGL – Above Ground Level.

Airspace – Categories of US Airspace A, B, C, D, E and G as well as controlled, uncontrolled and special use airspace are listed in the Federal Aviation Regulations, specifically 14 CFR 91.126 – 91.144.

AMA - American Academy of Model Aeronautics www.modelaircraft.org

CFR – Code of Federal Regulations of which Part 14 includes the FARs.

COA – Certificate of Authorization is a document issued to commercial drone operators specifying the operations they can conduct.

CRM – Crew Resource Management or "CRM"

Drone – A remotely controlled, pilotless aircraft.

FAA – Federal Aviation Administration.

FAR – Federal Aviation Regulations. Part 14 of the Code of Federal Regulations.

FSDO – Flight Standards District Office of the FAA.

GOM – General Operations Manual.

IFR – Instrument Flight Rules.

MSL – Mean Sea Level. Altimeters are set to indicate an aircraft altitude "MSL."

NAS – National Airspace System.

NOTAM – Notice to Airmen filed with the FAA AFSS (see AFSS) regarding procedures and hazards to flight. Drone flight operations must file these no earlier than 72 hours nor later than 24 hours before an intended drone operation.

P & L – Profit and Loss statement.

POI – Principal Operating Inspector is the Aviation Safety Inspector working for an FAA FSDO responsible for inspecting a particular flight operation or business.

SOP – Standard Operating Procedure.

sUAS – a small Unmanned Aerial System is one weighing between .55 pounds and 55 pounds. (see drone)

TFR – Temporary Flight Restriction.

VFR – Visual Flight Rules.

UAS – Unmanned Aerial System (see drone)

VLOS – Visual Line of Sight

VO – Visual Observer

Made in the USA
Middletown, DE
18 June 2021